THE OFFICIAL
COMPANION
SEASONS 1 & 2

24: **The Official Companion**
Seasons 1 & 2
ISBN 1 84576 313 0
ISBN-13 9781845763138

Published by Titan Books, a division of
Titan Publishing Group Ltd.
144 Southwark Street
London
SE1 0UP

First edition June 2006
10 9 8 7 6 5 4 3 2

The author would like to extend many thanks to the team at Fox: Day Vinson, Virginia King and Jacy Merson. During my own Jack Bauer-esque challenges over the past year, my eternal love and gratitude goes to all my unflagging cheerleaders including: Isabel and Gary, Denise, B, Pam, Bill, Jen, Lisa and Karen.
Thanks to my spiritual compasses Linda and Anne. To Martin, who took a chance on me and helped me realize my dream. And especially to my parents for believing in me and my mom, who shaped the writer in me long ago.
The publishers would like to thank the fantastic cast (both past and present) and crew of *24* for all their help with this book. A big thank you also to Day Vinson and Virginia King at Twentieth Century Fox.

What did you think of this book? We love to hear from our readers. Please email us at: **readerfeedback@titanemail.com** or write to us at the above address. You can also visit us at **www.titanbooks.com**

A CIP catalogue record for this title is available from the British Library.

Printed and bound in the USA.

The Official Companion
Seasons 1 & 2

Tara DiLullo

TITAN BOOKS

Contents

COUNTDOWN TO 24

Creating the Show

Time ticking by on a clock... minute-by-minute, second-by-second. It can be rather innocuous, mundane, even boring, but in the right context that ticking clock can become something else altogether: menacing, pulsing with life and fraught with potential danger — the greatest enemy of someone trying to stop events from leading to disaster. Put a person in jeopardy in a race against the clock and you can create narrative magic. In the past a few films, most memorably 1952's *High Noon*, utilized the concept of reflecting 'real-time' on screen to add gravity to their story, but episodic television had rarely explored the device. It took the vision of television producers Joel Surnow and Robert Cochran to mold the concept for the small screen and since then, a ticking digital clock has never been the same. In 2001, their contemporary spin on a race against time was developed into a television drama that has since become a true phenomenon, recognized around the world by its simple title — *24*.

As is the case with most 'big ideas', the inspiration for *24* came from the slightest of thoughts in, of all places, the bathroom of co-creator and executive producer Joel Surnow. "I was standing halfway between the sink and the shower in my bathroom, in the late spring of 2000," Surnow remembers with a smile. "I had just finished a season of the show I was doing at the time [*Special Unit 2*], and was obsessing over the fact that the next season of television I do is going to be another twenty-two episodes and there's no way around it. That's our business and it's just so *long*. I always wished that it could be shorter, so you could do other things. Of course, instead of thinking of something that would make it shorter, I thought of something that would take longer!

"I've got a semi-Tourette's kind of behavior when I look at numbers," he adds. "The first thing I always do

is to add them up and then divide them by three, as a thing to pass the time. Numbers are sort of a character in my life — I like numbers. I was thinking, 'twenty-two episodes... twenty-four hours in a day... twenty-two... twenty-four' and all of a sudden it just morphed into thinking, 'Could you do an entire season of television, twenty-four episodes, one-hour a piece?' And I went, 'Wow!' You know when you have an idea, you just sort of tingle a little bit and think, 'This is good!' I called Bob [Cochran] right away and said, 'Bob, I just came up with this thing, what do you think of it?' I pitched him the idea and he goes, 'It can't be done. You couldn't do an entire season in a day.' I said, 'Oh, you're probably right,' and took a shower, went about my business and put it out of my mind.

"But your subconscious does funny things, and my subconscious was obviously still wrangling with the idea," Surnow continues. "About two days later, I started to think, 'I bet you could do it. I don't know *how* you could do it, but you could do it.' I called Bob back — because he is my sounding board on everything — and I said, 'Let's sit down and see if we can crack this, because I think there is something special here.' We met halfway between his house and my house, which is an International House of Pancakes. You've gotta have the IHOP — another major player in this whole thing," he laughs. "We sat down and wondered what kind of story you could tell. We thought, 'Let's do a wedding — the day of a wedding. We could do a movie like *Lovers and Other Strangers* [1970], about all the crazy things that happen in the course of a wedding.' We pursued that idea for maybe an hour, but we just couldn't justify why someone would have to stay up twenty-four hours to organize a wedding."

The question remained: what would be the first reason somebody would have to stay up twenty-four hours?

Surnow lights up as he relates how he and Cochran found their answer: "Okay, something really bad is happening. What bad thing could happen? Let's throw this out: a President is going to be assassinated that day, and you are the federal agent in charge of making sure in that twenty-four-hour period he is not assassinated. That's good, but someone could split a watch with you. So we said, 'What if that's happening and at the same time your daughter disappears?' That seemed a preposterous idea, like too coincidental to do it, but it started getting us going. Then all of a sudden we started firing ideas. It unlocked us. The idea that this was a race against time, that the twenty-four hours wasn't just a day, but a race against time."

Surnow's partner, Robert Cochran continues, "We were looking for something that would be an edge-of-your-seat, adrenaline-filled thing, because you know the characters on the show are literally awake for twenty-four hours. It drove us toward models like *The Day of the Jackal* [1973] and *In the Line of Fire* [1993]. Assassination is one of the things that gives you an endpoint to move towards, and you stay awake and won't rest until the man is safe or the assassin is caught. The thing that was a challenge from a storytelling point of view, initially, was realizing that you can't really have twenty-four hours in a row of car chases and running around. There have to be personal stories as well, but how do you tell a personal story that has as much weight to it as that action story? With just about any personal crisis in your life, you can put it on hold for twenty-four hours."

The linchpin of the concept then became the character of Jack Bauer. A federal agent working on cases of national importance, Bauer was also dealing with a normal, messy family life that just about anyone watching the show could instantly relate to. Bauer's family dynamic became Surnow and Cochran's hook into the heart of the show. "One thing that I think most people understand and I think is true, is if someone has kidnapped one of your children, everything else pales," Cochran says. "We thought, 'What if we take this guy and on the one hand, charge him with the responsibility of stopping this assassination, and on the other hand, his child runs away that night?' As time goes on, he begins to suspect that she didn't just run away and she might be in trouble. *Then* you are putting him in

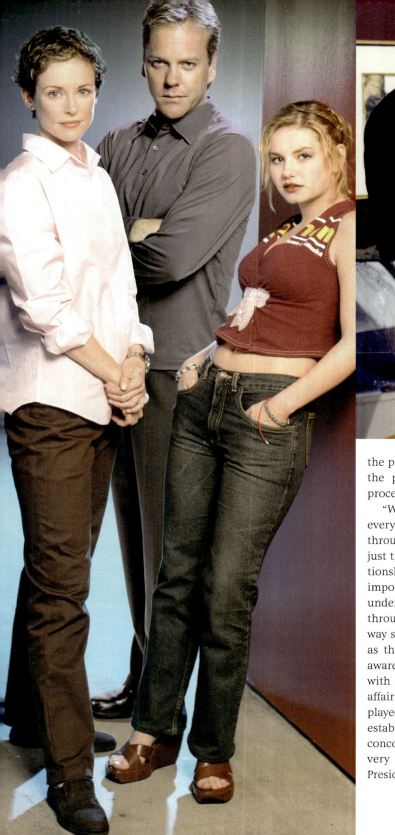

the place that gives him a personal story that matches the professional responsibility. That's the thought-process that went with it."

"We decided the key here is to raise the stakes on everything," Surnow continues. "So Jack Bauer is going through a marriage crisis and he and his wife [Teri] are just trying to get back together. He has a tenuous relationship with his daughter [Kim]. Again, what became important to everything was to keep the stuff bubbling under the surface. We knew we would be moving fast through the plot, but establishing the characters in a way so you know what their personal lives are like, so, as they are going through the motions, you are still aware he has a daughter at home, a wife he's dealing with and a girl at work [Nina Myers] who he had an affair with when he was separated. All those things played nicely, without ever having to be stated once you establish the context of the show. Off of that, we then concocted the story that we then pitched which was very close to how the pilot ended up — have a Presidential candidate [David Palmer] and make him black to raise the stakes. We had just gone through Rodney King. If LA had a black Presidential candidate assassinated, it could cause a race riot in the city, so let's keep the stakes up."

The pitch was now fully developed, and within a month Surnow and Cochran approached Fox Television to produce a pilot. "They bought it that day, which was really neat. They just loved it," Surnow remembers. "In fact, I'll tell you my track record in pilots: I had written eleven pilots in my career at that point and exactly zero of them got filmed. I was never successful in the pilot arena. I was always a good gun-for-hire who could work on or run a show, but I never seemed to have what it took to get my own stuff filmed. So it was a big deal. It was a great day. And then the work started," he laughs.

From the moment they began work on the script, they realized the real-time concept of the show would be the most difficult aspect for them to tailor to the standard television narrative structure. "From a technical point of view, storytelling on the screen is completely dependent most of the time on time cuts," Cochran explains. "Something happens and then you cut five minutes later,

five hours later or five days later, whatever it is. People are used to that. But with this format that we were trying to use — an example I always like to give is if you put a guy on a plane in Los Angeles and fly him to New York, on any other show or movie, he can be there in the next scene. On this show, he's on that plane for five episodes. So if you are going to do that, you have to come up with five episodes of stuff for that guy to do on a plane — and that's not easy to do," he laughs. "So we can't use time cuts, and what we realized we would have to do is have multiple storylines. The storylines function basically as time cuts for each other, by jumping from one to another. Jack has to get someplace, but we don't want to be in the car with him the whole time, so we cut to Kim. Eventually, we'll get back to Jack when he shows up where he was going. Juggling those storylines became our substitute for time cuts. We had Jack, his daughter, and the assassin to follow, and then we thought we would make a character of the target — which in *The Day of the Jackal* and *In the Line of Fire*, they didn't. We gave the Presidential candidate a story. The last one we thought of was a wife for Jack, who is a little irritated with him because she doesn't realize what he is facing. She goes

out into the city to try and find her daughter, which most mothers would do. So we had those five people, whose points of view we could follow. Juggling those stories was on one hand a solution for the time cut problem, but they were also their own challenge because keeping those balls in the air was, and is, the challenge of the whole format."

Surnow and Cochran were able to iron out their narrative issues for the pilot script, which they completed in October 2000. In late January 2001, the show dubbed *24* was picked up by Fox and went into production that summer. Set for a September 2001 début, *24* hit its first huge stumbling block with the terrorist attacks on the United States on 9/11. The nation, shell-shocked by the tragic events, retreated from difficult television en masse, leaving Fox wondering what to do with their intense drama starring Kiefer Sutherland as an agent for the fictional Counter Terrorism Unit (CTU) of Los Angeles.

Surnow admits they were genuinely worried about their future. "We didn't know what was going to happen.

But we had already finished four or five shows and had had a really great response from the studio and network, so they weren't ready to dump it. They made us change the explosion of the plane [in the pilot], and cut that back. Fortunately, it didn't seem to matter because we are still fiction, and I think there is now some curiosity about what anti-terrorist people do, as they are becoming a more important part of our lives." On 6 November 2001, *24* débuted, starting the clock at midnight. It was quickly embraced by audiences and critics alike.

Surnow and Cochran hired Howard Gordon as a fellow executive producer to help them plot the season, which Surnow admits quickly unraveled before them in the writers' room. "The fact of the matter is that what we set out to be a twenty-four-episode story, which was the assassination attempt on David Palmer, played out in seven episodes. In episode seven, the attempt on his life happens and that's when we said, 'Holy crap! We are screwed! We have another seventeen episodes to fill and we've just dispatched with our main story,'" he says, laughing. "We realized what works for a two-hour movie, doesn't work for a twenty-four-hour movie, and all these things that are interesting, if you play them out for three hours, you've exhausted the drama. So we needed to construct the show in a whole different way."

As they plotted the season, Surnow explains that a very organic approach began to guide the team, with two issues actually defining the show for them — the impact of 9/11 on the series, and the decision to kill Jack Bauer's wife in the season finale. "The first season lived in the world of fiction, and the second season lived in the world of post-9/11 America and it has ever since. The world of terrorism has invaded our lives and you can't cheat it and do silly stories about Neo-Nazis and say 'This is really the big threat to America' anymore. Whereas the inspiration for season one came from movies like *The Day of the Jackal* and *Three Days of the Condor* [1975], the inspiration for seasons two, three, four and five is 9/11."

The other moment of clarity for the series came in the choice to have Jack's CTU partner and former lover, Nina Myers, kill Teri Bauer. Surnow admits that action "defined the show as a tragedy. It was the pivotal moment of the whole series. *24 is* a tragedy. You get the bad guy but you pay the price, and if you look at every season, that's what happens." But deciding to actually go there became a bit of a battle, as executive producer and showrunner Howard Gordon reveals: "It was not a popular choice as far as the network was concerned. So much so that we actually shot it both ways, but we knew in our hearts that this had to be, because there was nowhere else to take it. The next year they would be happy and living in Tarzana and there's no drama there. Most importantly, she had to be sacrificed so that Jack Bauer was in a different emotional state for the second year."

In a shock for the critics, who argued that the show's crazy concept couldn't last more than one season, *24* was duly picked up for another year, but there were lessons to be learned. "We did a fairly sober report card on season one and we decided that we hadn't had a story that really sustained twenty-four episodes," Surnow admits. "We repeated ourselves a lot. Kim got grabbed again in the second half of the season. We didn't have what we felt was a full story. We had parts of stories and it was cobbled together. Having said that, we were really proud of the first half of that season because that was really the best place we've ever put Jack — choosing my family or my country. We knew we couldn't do that again. We decided we needed to now deal with the reality of terrorism, and a story that could sustain more than six or seven episodes."

Season two pushed forward eighteen months into the future with Jack Bauer estranged from his daughter, and the threat of a nuclear bomb being detonated in Los Angeles by a terrorist group from the Middle East. "The idea of someone smuggling a nuclear bomb into the United States seemed like a natural choice," Surnow explains. "It was not difficult to come up with the antagonist, or the actions of the antagonist. Obviously, all the other aspects, Jack being out of CTU and having to readjust to his daughter and get that relationship working again, all added a nice flavor. In the first season, he is trying to get his family together and in a strange way, in the second season, he is trying to get his family together and overcome the death of his wife. The real key for us in the second season was that the bomb detonated in episode fifteen, so we were already eight episodes further down the line than we were for that pivotal point in season one. We came up with the idea that someone was trying to pin the blame on a certain government in the Middle East and we were about to start a war. Then the invoking of the Twenty-fifth Amendment and that whole Palmer plotline really became a full complimentary story, and we were able to

keep the stakes high for the second half of the season."

"My favorite season is year two," Cochran states. "I think as a storyteller, I really enjoyed being able to connect the storylines. There were two phases to it: before the bomb went off, and after the bomb went off, and in that sense I felt it was a very cleanly structured season. You had the bomb, and then trying to stop the retaliatory war. They were two big chunks, and each chunk was organized very well around those ideas. I felt they were very strong and the second one actually flowed from the first one."

Reflecting on the first two years of *24*, Surnow is still very proud of what they were able to shape and create from an idea with such humble beginnings. Those first two seasons quickly established the show as a blockbuster hit, and laid solid foundations for the years to come. "In the first season, there were no stakes to the average citizen. The second season really got people going because they felt the fear. We felt like that's *24*. It sounds kind of comic-booky, but it's really Jack Bauer saving the world." **24**

My Name is Jack Bauer

Strip away the real-time concept of *24*, lose the incredible threats of epic proportion and the smaller-scale personal dramas, shed the car chases, the adrenaline-fueled action sequences and killer cliffhangers — and what's left? Just the key ingredient that makes all of those disparate elements gel to create a plausible world that audiences willingly accept and are thoroughly addicted to — Jack Bauer. As played by actor Kiefer Sutherland, Bauer has become a rarity on television: a character that is, on one hand, an unequivocal hero and patriot for his country, yet on the other, a very human man who fails as impressively in his personal life as much as he succeeds in saving the world time after time. Over the years, Sutherland has crafted Bauer into a man of action who exudes the tangible bite of world-weariness and sorrow. Despite his calling, his first loyalty lies with his family — the very thing he is asked to sacrifice time and time again to protect his country. That constant push and pull on Bauer has kept the character firmly grounded in reality, despite the incredible situations in which he finds himself immersed each "very bad" day. It's the connection that brings the audience back each week — not only to see how it ends, but where it will leave Jack once again.

In reality, for Sutherland, Jack Bauer is arguably the best match of man to role he has found in his twenty-plus years as an actor. Both men are survivors, family men and dedicated to their jobs. But Bauer also represents a rebirth in career for Sutherland that he admits has humbled him, especially at this stage of his life. The son of respected actors Donald Sutherland and Shirley Douglas, Kiefer was born in London, England in 1966, but was primarily raised in Canada. He jumped into acting in his teens and made a splash with the Canadian drama *The Bay Boy* in 1984. Sutherland modeled in New York City for a time and then relocated to Los Angeles,

where he made his mark in Hollywood playing memorable villain roles in *The Lost Boys* (1987), *Stand By Me* (1986), and *Flatliners* (1990). He spent the late eighties and early nineties in a variety of high profile films such as *Young Guns* (1988), *A Few Good Men* (1992), and *The Cowboy Way* (1994), before the roles of choice began to dry up. Sutherland was admittedly disenfranchised with the direction of his 'Hollywood' career, and in the late nineties refocused on smaller, more creative independent films like *The Vanishing* (1993), *Freeway* (1996) and *Dark City* (1998). He even left California for a time to join the rodeo circuit, where he became a respected bull roper.

Acting eventually lured him back to Los Angeles and in early 2001, Sutherland was offered the lead role in a new television series created by Joel Surnow and Robert Cochran...

Reflecting back on that initial meeting, Sutherland remembers, "I'd never done television before, so they didn't really pitch me the show. We just dealt with the pilot script. Joel and Bob had come across this really fantastic idea." Surnow and Cochran's words were enough to sell the actor on the concept, as he recognized the originality of the show and the depth of the character being offered to him. "Stephen Hopkins, who directed the pilot [and many other episodes in the first season], had also never done television before. We had known each other for a very long time and I had an incredible amount of faith in him.

"The reality of the real-time aspect of the show really didn't hit me until we started shooting," Sutherland continues. "It was a hypothetical to me. Everybody had their own version and their own idea of how it would work, so that wasn't a major factor in taking the role. The major factor was that I liked the character. I loved the dynamic of a man who, on a professional level, was

given so much responsibility: the safety of a future President of the United States, unraveling this terrorist plot and protecting this nation on such a level. Then counterbalanced with that was the fact that he was coming out of a very difficult time in his marriage and was having difficulty with his seventeen-year-old daughter. Those were things I could absolutely relate to. I loved the fact that he wasn't perfect — and that was all within the context of the pilot."

Having never committed to such a potentially long-term project, Sutherland admits the idea of being rooted to a series did concern him: "I found that a real challenge. What I hadn't understood, because I hadn't done television, was that when I go from film to film, it's very easy to make one or two very bold choices to differentiate characters, or to decide to choose a different story. So one film can be an action film and in the next one, you could be a man dying of AIDS. Those are very contrasting choices and very obvious. But the micro-management of a character like Jack over the five years that I've been doing this has been the greatest challenge I've ever had as an actor. To make

fifteen to twenty small choices that can ultimately, over a long period of time, have a cumulative effect has been the greatest learning experience that I've had as an actor to this date in my career."

That discovery began for the actor when he slipped into 'Day One' Jack Bauer, and Sutherland admits the opening year truly presented him with a learning curve, firstly in terms of just working on a series and then finding Jack as a character. The idea of considering long-term success for *24* wasn't even on his radar. "When you start, you would be foolish to even hope for that kind of success," the actor smiles. "We got picked up for the pilot and that was fantastic, then we had thirteen episodes to do and we focused on that. When we got picked up for the final eleven, we were just worried about how to complete that. We have operated as a group in many ways out of fear, which I think is one of the most powerful motivators and one of the most creative motivators. We got picked up from season to season and it's made us a little scared because we love making the show, but I think it's made us really edgy and it's made us fight — and I

wouldn't want it any other way."

Sutherland has taken that edge and used it to inspire his performance too. "Obviously, the show is a fantasy and it has to be made very clear that it's a fantasy, but within the context of that, you are going to try to do as much as you can to create a kind of reality that will allow an audience to suspend their own." Drawing from his own life of well-documented ups and downs, the actor admits all of those experiences inform Jack Bauer too. "Yes, there have been aspects of my life where I have been very strong, where I have managed to do things that I simply know other people might not have been able to do. But there are also aspects of my life where I have been very weak, where I have not succeeded in what I've tried to accomplish," he offers frankly. "On some level, that is what I have identified with in this character — his rate of failure to his rate of success. So that is always what I have started at in my own head. In my imagination, if I could be as strong as I could be, then that's what this character is."

As an actor though, he finds the failures in Jack's life, like his broken relationship with his daughter in

Above:
Guest director Frederick K. Keller talks to Kiefer Sutherland.

the first two seasons, a great source of drama and moments to play. "Liken that to a parent," Sutherland says. "I don't know a single child who has gone through their life and has not, at some point, been truly disappointed by a parent. I think it's an absolutely important dynamic in a relationship between a child and a parent."

The dichotomy of the character — the kind of hero one would aspire to be, and yet also a flawed, troubled human being who can and does fail — is what appeals to Sutherland. "Jack Bauer, in a weird way, is on one level what we should expect of ourselves, and on another level what we should expect of others, and if you are going to be honest about the depth of that, he is going to let you down. And he has on some levels. It's an interesting area for him to go to, and to see how he comes out of it. I

think it's dangerous to get into a character that has a morality that is so pat that you subscribe to it."

In the first two establishing seasons of 24, Sutherland is consistent in pinpointing the family dynamic as his favorite aspect of the show's early development. The Bauer family unit, as dysfunctional as it may have been, was the core of Jack's humanity and the key into his character. "In season one, I thought there were wonderful scenes with Teri and Jack that were really well written. Just the reality of being a couple: there were moments that I thought were very powerful," he reflects, "especially when contrasted with her death." The actor found the season one finale, with Jack cradling his wife's dead body as he breaks down, deeply unsettling. It was a story decision that he admits did not sit well with him at first. "I fought it very hard,

losing a character like Teri, because I have watched television and I knew for a fact that you ran a very big risk of losing your audience that has stayed with you for twenty-four episodes in a row. You give them a mixed ending like that, and they might just say, 'Forget about it!' But I thought it was an incredibly bold choice on Joel and Bob's behalf. I'll be the first one to tell you I disagreed with it, but in hindsight, I think it actually anchored my perception of who the character is — somone for whom everything comes at a price. You can save the would-be President's life and you can save your daughter's life, but you are going to pay something — and he lost his wife. It's been a through line in the writing, and hopefully in my performance of that character. Nothing comes without a cost. No positive outcome comes for free. They stay true to that as writers, and that's really been the foundation of what this character

has gone through now over almost five seasons."

In the second season of the series, Jack is a widower, and again at odds with his daughter, Kim. "There is continuity to the character over time," says the actor. "Certainly, at the beginning of season two, you absolutely see the repercussions of Jack losing his wife and becoming estranged from his daughter. You see the impact of the year and a half that the two days are separated by, and you carry that over from season one to two." Sutherland cites a moment between Jack and Kim, towards the end of the second season, that stuck with him almost as strongly as Teri's death. Kim is on the run from Gary Matheson, the physically abusive father of the girl she looks after. Intent on killing Kim for her part in turning him in to the authorities, Matheson comes face-to-face with her in a harrowing situation where Kim has to defend herself. By phone,

Jack is the one to guide her in the act of shooting Matheson in order to save her own life. The moment still has deep resonance for the actor. "Having to tell your daughter to kill someone..." he sighs. "I have a daughter, who was the same age then as Kim. I couldn't imagine being stuck on the phone knowing there was someone in the house with my daughter, trying to kill her and I had to tell her to do such a thing." And yet the highly trained Jack Bauer *is* able to tell her, his cold professionalism overcoming his emotion: "Jack gets so crossed as a character that he tells her to shoot again, just to make sure. Somehow, he crossed the line with his own daughter, where he let go of his anger with that situation."

As he continues Bauer's journey as a character, Sutherland is quick to relate how his craft has developed over the years. "I've learned to trust myself as an actor — that my instincts are what they are for a reason. They are now very honed to this character so I should have faith in that. Trust is not something that an actor comes by easily, and I trust this crew and this writing staff and their perspective as well, which has allowed me to be more open to the collaborative process than at any other time in my career. I think the one great fear that really motivates us is that because we have had such phenomenal success not only with our audience, but on a critical level — and that's not something we take for granted either — we feel an incredible sense of responsibility to the people that have supported us. The chief aspect of that responsibility is that we'll make a commitment to you to maintain the quality of the show. Not even to make it better, but to maintain the quality from season one — and the second that starts to drop, we'd better stop doing it." 24

DAY ONE

Regular Cast:
Kiefer Sutherland (Jack Bauer)
Leslie Hope (Teri Bauer)
Elisha Cuthbert (Kimberly Bauer)
Sarah Clarke (Nina Myers)
Carlos Bernard (Tony Almeida)
Dennis Haysbert (Senator David Palmer)
Penny Johnson Jerald (Sherry Palmer)

12:00 am - 1:00 am

Director: Stephen Hopkins
Writers: Robert Cochran & Joel Surnow

Guest Cast: Karina Arroyave (Jamey Farrell), Mia Kirshner (Mandy), Rudolf Martin (Martin Belkin), Daniel Bess (Rick), Richard Burgi (Alan York)

> "Don't trust anyone… not even your own people. We've got to find the shooter Jack… whatever it takes." Richard Walsh

Timeframe   Key Events

12:00 A.M. CTU Agent Richard Walsh is alerted that an assassin is planning to kill Senator David Palmer, an African American running for President.

12:02 A.M. Agent Jack Bauer is at home with his wife, Teri, and daughter, Kim. Jack and Teri discover Kim has snuck out of the house. Jack gets a call from Nina Myers at CTU to come into work immediately.

12:09 A.M. Kim and her friend, Janet York, go to a furniture store to party with Dan and Rick. Jack arrives at CTU.

12:14 A.M. Walsh briefs Jack and his team (Nina, Tony Almeida and Jamey Farrell) about the assassination plan. Walsh takes Jack aside and tells him of a possible leak within CTU connected to the hit.

12:22 A.M. Martin Belkin, a foreign photographer, is flying to LA to meet Palmer for breakfast. Mandy, a fellow passenger, strikes up a conversation.

12:25 A.M. Nina confronts Jack about Walsh. District Director George Mason arrives to further brief Jack, but refuses to disclose his source about the Palmer case. Jack shoots him with a tranquilizer gun and orders Nina to dig up information about Mason.

12:38 A.M. Janet's father, Alan York, calls Teri about his missing daughter.

12:43 A.M. Senator Palmer gets a call from reporter Maureen Kingsley. He is angered by it, but doesn't share the details with his wife Sherry.

12:48 A.M. Alan and Teri decide to meet and look for their daughters. Kim asks to be dropped off at home.

12:52 A.M. Mandy and Martin have sex in the airplane bathroom. At CTU, Mason wakes up and Jack succeeds in blackmailing him. Mandy steals Martin's ID, primes a bomb and ejects herself safely from the plane before it explodes.

12:57 A.M. News hits of the plane disaster. Kim realizes she may be in danger.

Jack shoots George Mason with tranq gun.

Mandy detonates the plane bomb.

Kim realizes she's in trouble.

The first season of *24* starts at midnight, a reasonably logical jumping off point for the series format, but co-creator Robert Cochran says that choice created plenty of issues. "We decided to start the first episode at midnight because we thought it would be cool. We start shooting in the summer and on our show we need night, night, night, but in real life the days are long. It was a problem then because as the show goes on it starts to need daylight, but in real life the days become shorter; so we had to fight that all year long and that's why no season since season one has ever started at night or ever will. Now, the needs of our show fit what's happening outside more. I think it worked well the first year, but it was a production problem.

"Also, at that time there was talk of maybe shooting in Canada. We really can't because the show takes place in one day and so

the weather can't change drastically or it will look ridiculous. If you try to shoot in Vancouver or Toronto, you are going to have both snow and rain and if it happened all on the same day it would be silly. So that enabled us to say we really have to shoot in Southern California."

The pilot also introduced the concurrent storylines, one involving a mysterious call David Palmer receives. Co-creator Joel Surnow admits that call was an even bigger mystery to the writing staff. "Palmer gets that phone call and it's a big deal, like something terrible just happened. He excuses himself and walks onto the balcony and looks out on the city with a 'How am I going to handle this?' look. We had no idea what that was! We just knew we could drop it in and it would make people want to come back and find out what the mystery was. We didn't have it solved!"

Research Files

Counter Terrorist Unit (CTU): *24*'s CTU is a fictional elite branch of the Central Intelligence Agency (CIA) that is charged with investigating the activities of domestic and foreign terrorist groups and individuals operating within US borders, to ultimately prevent any terrorist attack on domestic soil. The CTU was created after the 1993 World Trade Center bombings, with its headquarters in Washington DC and field satellite operations in major cities where threats are likely, such as Los Angeles, California. CTU is comprised of a variety of agents, including investigators, intelligence experts, technical researchers, undercover ops, and tactical squads. They all work under a CTU director, in conjunction with the FBI, the Secret Service, the Justice Department, and any and all pertinent local authorities. In season one, Jack Bauer is the Special Agent in Charge of the Los Angeles Domestic Unit of CTU.

Additional Intel

Leslie Hope gets into the car in the pilot in an outfit consisting of a black denim jacket and blue shirt, that the actress did not like. So in the second episode, costume designer Jim Lapidus says he "cheated" and Teri gets out of the car wearing a gray silk sweater over a blue shirt.

1:00 am - 2:00 am

Director: Stephen Hopkins
Writers: Joel Surnow & Michael Loceff

Guest Cast: Michael Massee (Ira Gaines), Matthew Carey (Dan), Karina Arroyave (Jamey Farrell), Jacqui Maxwell (Janet York)

"She's fine. You know, Kim said she loved me. Kim never says that." Teri Bauer

Timeframe	Key Events

1:02 A.M. Mandy parachutes to safety. She buries Belkin's ID in a homing case. A car picks her up and then a motorcyclist appears and digs up the ID.

1:09 A.M. Walsh has a secret meeting downtown with Agent Baylor. Walsh is given a key card with embedded files referencing Palmer. Shots ring out. Baylor is killed and Walsh is wounded. Jack gets a call from Walsh for help.

1:17 A.M. Jack checks in with Teri on his way to Walsh. Kim realizes Janet has been drugged.

1:22 A.M. Mandy arrives at a remote desert house where Ira Gaines gives her a briefcase full of money. Mandy arranges for the ID to be dropped off.

1:23 A.M. Jack arrives to help Walsh and calls Nina for an entry code.

1:29 A.M. Ira introduces Mandy to Jonathan, a sniper transformed to look like Belkin.

1:31 A.M. Jack finds Walsh alive. They have a gun battle with three shooters, killing two. Jack cuts the finger off one to get his print.

1:36 A.M. The motorcyclist, Bridgit, pulls up at Gaines' house and demands $2 million for the ID.

1:42 A.M. Unable to get Jack, Teri calls Nina to get the furniture store-owner's name.

1:44 A.M. Palmer's children, Keith and Nicole, arrive. Palmer gets a call from his aide, Carl. He tells him about Maureen's call and they agree to meet.

1:53 A.M. As they leave the building downtown, Walsh is shot and he gives the key card to Jack to give to Jamey.

1:54 A.M. Jack scans the key card over to Jamey from his truck. Dan pulls over and forces Kim to call her mom saying everything is all right. She refuses and he smashes Janet's arm. She calls and tells her mom she loves her. Teri is alarmed.

1:59 A.M. Jamey sends Jack the source of the card — Nina. Jonathan does some target practice.

Agent Walsh and Agent Baylor are ambushed and shot.

Ira gives Mandy the briefcase.

A dying Walsh passes Jack the key card.

One of the production hallmarks of *24* is the unique insert-box editing style that shows all the multiple storylines on screen at once. A technique previously used in films like the original *Thomas Crown Affair*, co-creator Robert Cochran says the style that is now so synonymous with their show was something they fell into during post-production on the pilot. "The boxes came about in a funny way. We didn't think about them at all at first and then we started filming the pilot and watching dailies and saw there were *so* many phone calls. It's real because everybody lives on their phones nowadays and if you are a law enforcement type, you are on the phone even more, but we found it was pretty deadly watching people on the phone. The director, Stephen Hopkins, made sure people were at least on the move when they are on the phone: walking, driving, running or doing something else, so there is a sense of

Research Files

African American Presidential Candidate: Senator David Palmer of Maryland is the first African American candidate to run for President of the United States. Article Two of the United States Constitution requires that in order to become President, a candidate must be a natural-born citizen of the United States, at least thirty-five years old, and have been a resident of the United States for fourteen years. In reality, an African American has yet to run for President, but there have been a total of five African American senators in US history: Hiram Revels (elected 1870), Blanche K. Bruce (1875), Edward Brooke (1966), Carol Moseley Braun (1992) and Barack Obama (2005). Other African Americans of note in government include US Secretary of State, General Colin Powell (2001–2004), and the first black female Secretary of State, Condoleezza Rice (2005).

Additional Intel

All of the actors that make up the Bauer family unit — Kiefer Sutherland, Leslie Hope and Elisha Cuthbert — were either born or raised in Canada. Although born in London, England, Kiefer was raised primarily in Ontario; Leslie was born in Nova Scotia; while Elisha was born in Calgary.

energy. When it came time to cut the thing together, I think it was Stephen and the editor, Dave Thompson, who started thinking. 'Let's put two boxes on the screen so you can see both people at once and at least one will be moving.' That third box was the nice stroke, because you end up close up enough on a guy to see his emotions and you are also backed off to see what he is doing. Then we began to think that you don't have to limit the boxes to phone call scenes. Once we saw it on screen, we realized how well it fit the multiple storyline format because you could follow more than one story at a time; so that all came together, but not, I'm sorry to say, as something we sat down and played out before filming the show."

2:00 am - 3:00 am

Director: Stephen Hopkins
Writers: Joel Surnow & Michael Loceff

Guest Cast: Michael Massee (Ira Gaines), Mia Kirshner (Mandy), Vicellous Reon Shannon (Keith Palmer), Zach Grenier (Carl Webb)

"This is Almeida at CTU. Look, you better get down here fast... Jack Bauer needs to be relieved of his command." Tony Almeida

Timeframe — Key Events

2:00 A.M. Jack scans the finger to CTU. Teri calls Jack.

2:05 A.M. Ira orders Mandy to handle Bridgit. Sherry has no idea where David has gone.

2:08 A.M. Ira tells Dan he is running late. Janet is in terrible pain and Rick injects her with drugs.

2:14 A.M. Palmer pulls into a parking garage and has a run in with two thugs smashing cars.

2:17 A.M. Jack returns to CTU and distracts Nina so he can pass the key card to Jamey. He has her trace the source of the card — Nina's terminal.

2:27 A.M. At Ira Gaines' house, Mandy and Bridgit argue over the money. In the van, Kim convinces Janet they are in trouble. While Rick and Dan are distracted, the girls flee. At CTU, Jamey encourages Jack to limit Nina's access.

2:32 A.M. Kim and Janet run into a junkie who covers for them when Dan and Rick show up.

2:39 A.M. Palmer meets Carl and tells him about Maureen's accusation that Keith murdered Nicole's rapist seven years ago and covered it up. Carl agrees to take care of it as the Secret Service arrives, looking for Palmer.

2:43 A.M. Jack confronts Nina about the key card and she denies involvement. In the desert, Ira agrees to the women's demands.

2:52 A.M. Tony reads a memo announcing Walsh's death and he and Jamey follow up.

2:56 A.M. Jamey shows Jack and Nina the data she found on the key card. They establish Nina was with Jack when the data was gathered. Jack apologizes to Nina, but she is livid. Tony calls CTU Headquarters to let them know Jack needs to be relieved of his command.

2:57 A.M. Kim gets access to a phone and calls her mom. Teri calls 911. Still on the run, a car hits Janet and the boys recapture Kim.

Kim and Janet flee the boys.

David Palmer and Carl's secret meeting.

Janet is hit by a car.

Costume designer Jim Lapidus and costume supervisor Jean Rosone have been dressing the actors since the second episode (Rob Saduski costumed the pilot). With the intense continuity issues surrounding the format of the show, the duo explains that the first season in particular was rife with unexpected problems and challenges for their department. The difficulties specifically came out of the strict, real-time parameters of the show. In this episode, Rosone remembers, "We had a big problem with the girl who gets hit by the car, Janet. When they did the pilot, they had her in a little tank top and a miniskirt and flip-flops." Lapidus continues, "Now we are going to hit her with a car! How do you do that? Luckily, we had Kim's purse, which we called the 'magic bag' — anything could come out of that bag. It produced a sweatshirt long enough to cover this girl and cover some pads so she

could take a hit by the car. So now, from that, whenever we have new characters, we give them 'magic bags' so that when all of a sudden a writer says, 'He takes his gun' or 'He takes his cell phone...' at least there is something for them to take it out of, and it's been there all the time."

Rosone comments that the year-long costume decisions have become more intuitive now. "We have to walk a very fine line because we have to give them a character, without people noticing that they don't change their clothes." Lapidus concurs saying, "My challenge is that they walk into the room and the producers and the directors see the fitting and then I have to live with it for the rest of the year. The stress for Jean and I is that it has to be right the first time. You can't say after that first hour, 'Gee, I really hated the way she looked, go and change that outfit.'"

Research Files

Optical Scanners: Jack has a portable image scanner built into his truck for scanning images or photos (or, in this case, an actual fingerprint from a dead man's finger) that can be transmitted directly to CTU for analysis. Jack's scanner is a smaller version of a traditional desktop scanner found in many offices and is more efficient than handheld scanners, which are known for their inability to reproduce high quality scans for study. The resulting digital scan takes the image and divides it into a grid of boxes, each represented by either a zero or a one. Those boxes are created in a matrix, called a 'bit map', that can be stored, saved, processed in software systems and analyzed for minute details.

Additional Intel

In the late 1990s, *24* co-creators Joel Surnow and Robert Cochran both worked on the espionage television drama, *La Femme Nikita*. When *24* was picked up by Fox, they hired several actors and crew from *Nikita* including producer Michael Loceff, composer Sean Callery and director Brad Turner.

3:00 am - 4:00 am

Director: Winrich Kolbe
Writer: Robert Cochran

Guest Cast: Vicellous Reon Shannon (Keith Palmer),
Zach Grenier (Carl Webb), Richard Burgi (Alan York),
Xander Berkeley (George Mason)

"Off the record, what is so special about Jack Bauer?" George Mason

Timeframe	Key Events

3:00 A.M. Janet is left for dead in the street.

3:03 A.M. Jack explains Walsh's death to Nina. He says Nina and Jamey are the only people he trusts.

3:04 A.M. Palmer returns. Sherry informs him of the assassination attempt. Jamey decrypts an address from the key card. Mason arrives at CTU and authorizes a lockdown. Jack sneaks out.

3:13 A.M. Nina confronts Tony about calling in Mason.

3:17 A.M. The Secret Service explains to Palmer the connection between the plane crash and the threat on his life. Palmer refuses to cancel the breakfast, an important event in his campaign.

3:19 A.M. In the van, Kim begs Dan and Rick to go back for Janet. Dan agrees so he can make sure she is dead. Rick tapes Kim up.

3:21 A.M. Teri and Alan get pulled over by a cop. The van passes right by them.

3:29 A.M. Jack arrives at the key card address. Jack sees a man and gives chase. Policewoman Jessie Hampton assists Jack and they have a shootout with the suspect.

3:36 A.M. Dan prepares to shoot Janet, but an ambulance arrives so they quickly leave.

3:40 A.M. Nina tells Jamey not to tell Mason anything.

3:42 A.M. Sherry confronts David about his secret calls. He explains Maureen intends to report about Keith's alleged murder cover-up. Keith's therapist, George Ferragamo, claims Keith confessed. David worries it may be true. The shooter, Penticoff, takes Jessie Hampton hostage.

3:44 A.M. A police helicopter arrives as backup for Jack and Hampton.

3:52 A.M. Jack tricks Penticoff and there's a fracus, a shot is fired and Hampton is killed. Teri and Alan race to the hospital. Mason ends the lockdown when Jack is found. The guys give Kim to Ira Gaines.

3:59 A.M. Penticoff yells to Jack "If you ever want to see your daughter again, get me out of this!" In a panic, Jack follows the squad car.

Sherry informs David of the assassination attempt.

Jack and the shooter have a stand off.

Penticoff takes Hampton hostage.

When working out the major storylines for season one, Joel Surnow and Robert Cochran knew that Jack's dedication to protecting his family would be the true motivating factor for all his actions during the entire season. The fact that Teri and Kim were in jeopardy too, while he was trying to save Senator Palmer's life, would be the heart of the series. Working out the dynamics of the Bauer family early on, Surnow says they played around initially with a range of ages for Jack's daughter. "I thought, if you had a teenage daughter, you had a more complicated story. If you have a five-year-old, first of all, you have a five-year-old actor. You don't really have an actor who is developed enough to be able to do anything dramatic, so they really just become symbolic of something. They don't become players in a game. I think a man who has been through a separation and is dealing with his teenage daughter... Bob and I both had teenage daughters ourselves at the

Research Files

Encryption: The key card that Walsh gives to Jack is encrypted with hidden data that needs to be deciphered in order to gain access to it. The art of encryption has been used to protect sensitive communications for centuries, with governments primarily using the process to protect their vital information from enemies. In the last thirty years, encryption has gone high-tech with the information age and the integration of computers for daily business needs, like Internet e-commerce, online banking and mobile-phone communications. Encryption ensures safety for individual users and their PIN or account information, as well as for huge corporations or government agencies with vast databases full of highly sensitive data and personal information archives. On the flip side, encryption has become particularly vulnerable to aggressive hackers in recent years, leading to constant concern that effective encryption will become harder and harder to accomplish, allowing criminal activity to rise, with more breaches in sensitive security, e-commerce and healthcare databases.

Additional Intel

Co-creator Joel Surnow reveals that the name of Kiefer's character was originally Jack Barrett. However, Surnow and Cochran didn't love the name Barrett and there happened to be an executive over at Imagine Entertainment named Elaine Bauer who came to mind, so they changed it from Barrett to Bauer.

time, so there was more complicated stuff there that we had dealt with firsthand too."

Finding the right Kim Bauer fell to the casting director for the pilot, Debi Manwiller. Seventeen-year-old Elisha Cuthbert had just moved to Los Angeles from Canada when her tape reached the *24* casting desk. Manwiller says finding the right age fit for Kim was a big issue. "If you look at somebody to last the life of a series, you have to be very careful when casting a teenager. At the time I didn't ever consider that our show might not be set in successive years, so for us, jumping two or three years could have been a problem. Also, Kiefer is young so you can't link him with someone who is twenty-two years old either because what would that look like five years down the road?" So in look, chemistry and talent, it ended up Cuthbert was the perfect fit.

4:00 am - 5:00 am

Director: Winrich Kolbe
Writer: Chip Johannessen

Guest Cast: Michael Massee (Ira Gaines), Tanya Wright (Patty Brooks), Glenn Morshower (Aaron Pierce), Daniel Bess (Rick)

"Well Dan, I'll tell you, either you're dead or you're not dead, there's no such thing as sorta dead. Here, let me show you." Ira Gaines

Timeframe · Key Events

4:00 A.M. Janet is prepped for surgery.

4:02 A.M. Jack chases the squad car. Ira tells Dan and Rick to pick up their money at the compound.

4:06 A.M. Sherry asks David not to tell Nicole about Keith.

4:09 A.M. Jack calls Nina for help. Nina needs Tony's help. Mason arrives at the police station.

4:16 A.M. Mason confronts Jack about Walsh. Jack explains the Penticoff connection. Ira pulls a gun on Kim.

4:19 A.M. Palmer phones Maureen for a meeting. Mason says Penticoff will only talk to Jack. In the interrogation room, Jack whispers something to the suspect and he goes nuts. Penticoff demands his phone call.

4:23 A.M. Penticoff has Jack's phone number hidden in his mouth and calls Jack. He tells Jack he is expected at a pay phone in twenty minutes and if he isn't there, Kim will die. Jack has Nina track the pay phone and set up a trace.

4:29 A.M. Jack approaches Hampton's partner for another chance with Penticoff. The cop agrees. Jack and Penticoff tussle. Jack is thrown out, but he slips Penticoff an access card.

4:32 A.M. Palmer meets Maureen. He asks about her motives and she admits she has a handwriting match to Keith from the night of the murder.

4:40 A.M. Palmer wakes up his son and confronts him. Keith won't tell him anything.

4:43 A.M. Jack and Penticoff escape.

4:47 A.M. Jack and Penticoff arrive at the pay phone. A cell phone planted in the booth rings, bypassing the trace. Penticoff is instructed to dispose of a body in the trunk of a car. Jack fears it is Kim.

4:53 A.M. They find the car and the body is a John Doe. Mason arrives. Penticoff is arrested, and Jack explains everything and is released.

4:57 A.M. Jack calls Teri.

4:59 A.M. Dan admits that Janet is alive. Ira shoots Dan and 'promotes' Rick. Janet flatlines.

Janet is prepped for surgery.

Penticoff reveals Jack's note.

David Palmer and his son talk.

It was during Elisha Cuthbert's first trip to Los Angeles that she was cast as Kim Bauer in the *24* pilot. Cuthbert remembers, "*24*, I think, was the twentieth show I auditioned for that season, so it was really my last chance before it was time to pack up and go home. So there were a lot of feelings going on besides the fact that when I read the script, I just thought, 'What is this?' It was really interesting.

"When I think back on it now, the pilot felt like its own entity," she continues. "We didn't know if we were going to get picked up or continue shooting the show. I didn't even realize the opportunity was there to keep shooting it and looked at the pilot as a one-shot deal. So I didn't really pay attention to the wardrobe or the details with my hair. I had no idea the character was going to end up in this mayhem!"

The actress admits the first season was an intense learning

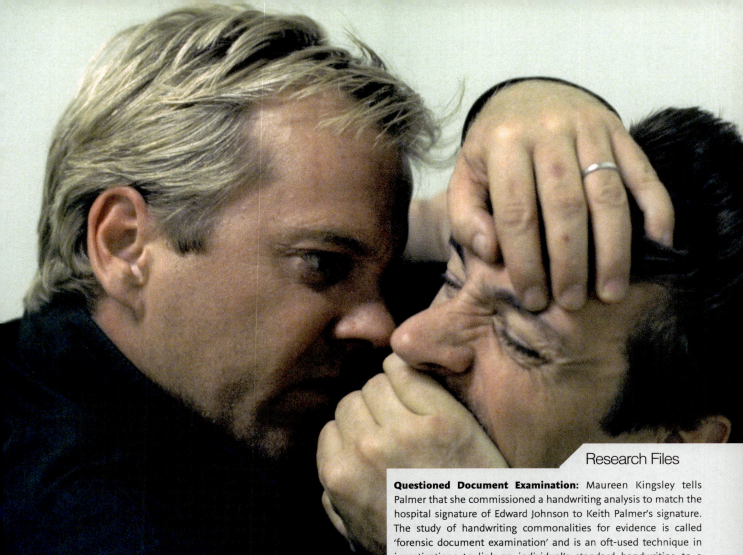

Research Files

Questioned Document Examination: Maureen Kingsley tells Palmer that she commissioned a handwriting analysis to match the hospital signature of Edward Johnson to Keith Palmer's signature. The study of handwriting commonalities for evidence is called 'forensic document examination' and is an oft-used technique in investigations to link an individual's standard handwriting to a piece of specific evidence with similar handwriting properties. The questioned and known items are analyzed and broken down into directly perceptible characteristics (for example specific cursive shapes, crossings or printing traits). Evaluations of the similarities and differences are studied, with a focus on any particular handwriting uniqueness and frequencies, from which a determination is made on any matching conclusions.

experience. "It was a crazy ride of running around and night shoots. It was my first real experience of putting in twelve-hour days that started at five pm and ended at five am. I was like, 'Wow, this isn't as glamorous as I thought it was going to be,' as I'm getting duct taped and thrown in the back of a van," she laughs. "But I was excited because it felt very authentic as we were actually participating in all the action. It was my first real taste of that caliber of show with that kind of budget; it was an exciting time to just be around all of it. For me, as I was getting sent all these scripts full of all this crazy stuff, it was just about making sure that I made it come across as real as possible and made my storyline make sense with the rest of the show."

Additional Intel

According to composer Sean Callery, the final edit of the *24* pilot was the twenty-fourth version and it was locked on 24 April 2001. Callery has worked on the series since the pilot and received an Emmy for his work in 2003 for Outstanding Music Composition for a Series (Dramatic Underscore).

5:00 am - 6:00 am

Director: Bryan Spicer
Writer: Howard Gordon

Guest Cast: Michael Massee (Ira Gaines), Daniel Bess (Rick), Karina Arroyave (Jamey Farrell), Eric Balfour (Milo Pressman), Kim Miyori (Dr. Collier)

"Jack's more uptight than the rest of us."
Teri Bauer

Timeframe   Key Events

5:00 A.M. Janet is revived. Nina meets Jack with a helicopter.

5:04 A.M. Ira has Rick dig a hole for Dan. Kim asks Rick to help her escape.

5:06 A.M. Palmer confronts Carl about his part in the cover up. Carl admits Keith said it was self-defense, so he helped him. Palmer fires Carl, who says David should talk to his wife too.

5:14 A.M. Kim helps Rick dig the grave.

5:16 A.M. Jack arrives at the hospital. Jack meets Alan and starts grilling him.

5:19 A.M. Palmer confronts Sherry about Carl. She admits the whole family was in on it. Palmer says she is too ambitious and she says she was keeping Keith out of jail.

5:27 A.M. Kim and Rick bond. Jack calls Nina about the John Doe.

5:29 A.M. Jack pulls Teri aside and explains the Palmer and Kim kidnapping connection.

5:37 A.M. Jamey is reassigned to the John Doe. Palmer wakes up his Chief of Staff, Mike Novick, to explain the situation and that he wants to go public.

5:39 A.M. Novick tells Palmer he will need his family to support him at the breakfast.

5:42 A.M. Jack gets a call from Ira directing him to leave the building. Alan visits Janet alone and suffocates her.

5:51 A.M. Ira instructs Jack to get into a silver Taurus, put on an earpiece and then throw out his cell phone. Ira puts Kim on the phone to prove she is alive.

5:54 A.M. Alan lies, telling Teri that Janet gave him an address where Kim may be. He offers to drive her there. Teri calls Jack but there's no answer.

5:57 A.M. Nina identifies the body as an Alan York from the Valley. Teri calls Nina looking for Jack, but Nina thought he was with Teri. She leaves the York info with Teri, who now knows the man she's with is not York.

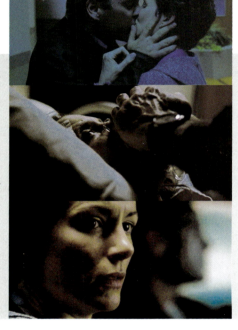

Jack and Teri reunite.

Kevin suffocates Janet.

Teri realizes she's in danger.

This episode was executive producer Howard Gordon's first script for the series, although the revelation of Alan York as Kevin Carroll was a story point that came prior to his time on the show. Joel Surnow remembers, "When we were doing the pilot and starting to think about where these story points might go, I remember walking into Bob's office and he had one of those magic marker boards where he had blocked off the first six episodes. We were still shooting the pilot, but he was starting to do some general big picture thinking. I think he said something like, 'What if Alan York isn't Alan York and this guy kills this girl here in episode four?' So that was a Bob Cochran story idea well before we were even breaking the story of the season."

Gordon admits this script helped him unlock the intricacies of the show. "The show constantly teaches you things and humbles you. One epiphany in my first script was this wonderful reversal

Microtransmitter Telephones: The nifty earpiece Ira Gaines provides to Jack for unobtrusive communication is a technology close to becoming reality for everyone. The television industry has been using wired and wireless earpieces called IFB (interruptible feedback) devices for many years, which allow the on-camera talent to hear their producer or director in their ear during a broadcast. Cell phone users now utilize a version of the technology with wireless hands-free headsets or ear buds that allow them to hear and speak to a caller without holding the phone to their ear. New technology research predicts the small earpiece technology reflected in the episode will be a reality soon, and will also exist in alternative devices like watches, jewelry, apparel buttons or cuff links.

Additional Intel

The first season of *24* was nominated for ten Emmy awards including: Outstanding Drama Series, Outstanding Lead Actor for a Drama Series (Sutherland), Writing, Directing, Casting, Underscore for a Series, Art Direction, Editing (two nominations) and Sound Mixing. It won the awards for Writing and Editing.

where Alan York, the father, was not who he advertised to be. I knew I'd have a moment where Teri gets a call and learns that the guy she's driving with isn't who he says he is, and I was looking forward to writing that. The second thing was finding out what you could do in an hour. Not much can really happen in one hour, so Kim and her boyfriend, who had deceived her, had to bury his friend, who had been killed. Just the simple act of digging a hole and covering it up, I knew would take about an hour. That to me was very emblematic of what the show was about — very simple actions, but complicating them emotionally. In that time, while they are doing this physical action of burying a friend, she ends up convincing this guy to help her escape. You learn a little bit about them and so, in a way, as they are digging and burying the friend, they are also digging deeper and finding out about each other."

Jack Bauer

CTU Missions:

Team Leader – Operation Proteus

Section Captain – Hotel Los Angeles attack

Experience:

CTU – Head of Field Ops, Los Angeles Domestic Unit

Los Angeles PD – Special Weapons and Tactics

Education:

Basic SWAT School – LASD

University of California (Berkeley) – Master of Science, Criminology and Law

University of California (Los Angeles) – Bachelor of Arts, English Literature

Special Forces Operations Training Course

Military:

US Army – Combat Applications Group, Delta Force Counter Terrorist Group

Personal:

Married – Teri Bauer

Daughter – Kimberly Bauer

6:00 am - 7:00 am

Director: Bryan Spicer
Writer: Andrea Newman

Guest Cast: Michael Massee (Ira Gaines), Karina Arroyave (Jamey Farrell), Silas Weir Mitchell (Eli Stram), Richard Burgi (Alan York/Kevin Carroll)

"You've got a gun on me Jack. I don't think it gets any worse." Nina Myers

Timeframe   Key Events

6:00 A.M. Jonathan prepares for the Palmer breakfast. Ira orders Jack to return to CTU. Milo, a CTU freelance contractor, is close to cracking the key card.

6:05 A.M. Palmer asks his son to stand by him, but an angry Keith refuses.

6:08 A.M. Jack is told about the Alan York ID. Ira instructs Jack to swap the key cards. Ira calls Kevin (the fake Alan) to warn him. In the car, Teri fakes sickness and runs. Kevin hears Ira's message and chases Teri. She knocks him out with a rock.

6:17 A.M. Teri ties Kevin to a tree. Her cell phone doesn't work. Rick asks to leave, but Ira has more work for him.

6:19 A.M. Jack realizes CTU is bugged with video cameras.

6:21 A.M. Palmer talks to Nicole. Jack spills a cup at Milo's station and swaps the key cards.

6:29 A.M. Kevin wakes up and tells Teri that Kim will die if he doesn't deliver Teri to his boss.

6:31 A.M. Ira has Jack call the Secret Service to get access to Palmer's breakfast. Rick and Kim plan an escape. Milo figures out that Jack swapped the key cards. Nina confronts Jack. He forces a jacket on her, holds a gun to her back and they leave CTU.

6:42 A.M. Teri calls Jack — no answer. Teri calls Nina at CTU and Jamey answers. Jamey promises to send help.

6:43 A.M. Sherry wants to blackmail Maureen. 'CTU agents' find Teri and then kidnap her and release Kevin.

6:49 A.M. Nina drives while Ira directs Jack in his ear. Nina is worried Jack is a rogue.

6:54 A.M. Jack has Nina stop the car. Obeying Ira, he shoots her. Nina rolls down a hill.

6:57 A.M. Kim and Rick almost escape, but Kim sees her mom and can't leave her.

6:59 A.M. Tony scans video footage of Jack and Nina and wonders why Jack put a flak jacket on her. Nina regains consciousness.

Teri attacks Kevin with a rock.

Jack turns a gun on Nina.

Jack shoots Nina.

During the first third of the season, Teri Bauer was primarily occupied with trying to track down Kim with the assistance of Janet's father, Alan York. It wasn't until the twist revealing that Alan was actually Kevin Carroll, Ira Gaines' henchman, that actress Leslie Hope got an inkling of where her character was headed. "Honestly, I thought it would be a show starring Kiefer Sutherland and we'd have this cute teenage daughter and if we got picked up, I would show up once a week and say, 'Honey, when are you coming home?'" she laughs. "That's really what I thought the extent of it would be, with maybe a few shots of me pacing in the kitchen or something."

In fact, the story put Teri in the physical mix too, something Hope was eager to explore. "I'm not somebody you would consider to be a shrinking violet, so maybe that was an indication to the

writers that it would be a good way to go." In this episode, Teri got to attack Kevin on a hilltop, which she did successfully, if not prettily. Laughing, Hope remembers, "I adore Richard Burgi, but I couldn't wait to crack him on the back of the head with that rock. It was one of my best moments on the show! As fantastic as some of those situations on *24* were and are, the thing that I liked was that it stayed grounded in some kind of reality, so even though I moved into some action-oriented type scenarios, I didn't become a superhero. I couldn't all of a sudden throw a punch like nobody's business or take on five guys in ninja outfits in a kung-fu battle. It still maintained a thread of reality, and everything they threw my way, I could track it and make sense of it. I was never in a situation on that show, believe it or not, where I was saying, 'My character would never do this!' Everything seemed to be in the realm of possibility, considering the circumstances and the plot."

Research Files

Flak Jacket: Jack forces Nina to put on a flak jacket that will ultimately save her life when he shoots her at close range near the end of the hour. The Wilkinson Sword Company invented flak jackets during World War Two, to protect Royal Air Force crewmen from German shrapnel bombs. Created with a material called ballistic nylon, developed by Dupont, the jackets also utilized titanium plates. Over the decades, Dupont expanded on their research and in 1971 marketed an even more advanced protective material known as Kevlar, from which modern bulletproof vests are made. The engineered fiber is five times stronger, ounce for ounce, than steel, but with about half the density of fiberglass. While the term 'bulletproof' is often associated with protective vests, it's not entirely accurate, considering some ammunition is made specifically to breach Kevlar.

Additional Intel

According to costume designer Jim Lapidus, Jack Bauer made twelve clothing changes during the first season of *24*. Most of those changes occured at CTU because he had locker access in his office, making the switches convenient and plausible.

7:00 am - 8:00 am

Director: Stephen Hopkins

Writers: Joel Surnow & Michael Loceff

Guest Cast: Michael Massee (Ira Gaines), Daniel Bess (Rick), Jackie Debatin (Jessica Abrams), Jesse D. Goins (Alan Hayes)

> "You better put that away. Someone could get hurt." Jonathan, the sniper

Timeframe   Key Events

7:00 A.M. Nina starts walking. Palmer tells his family he will admit the truth at the breakfast. Jonathan arrives at the breakfast. Ira directs Jack to pick up a briefcase and go to the breakfast. Ira lets Jack hear Teri's voice.

7:08 A.M. Ira contacts Jamey and tells her Nina is dead.

7:11 A.M. Teri is brought to the shed where Kim is being held. Kim is upset to learn that Janet is dead.

7:17 A.M. Nina finds a phone and calls Jamey, but there's no answer. She calls Tony asking for Jamey, but he catches Jamey in a lie about where Nina is. He tells Nina and she realizes Jamey is "dirty". Tony sends a car for Nina.

7:25 A.M. Jack arrives and passes security. Jack makes eye contact with Palmer. 'Belkin' is introduced to the Senator.

7:29 A.M. Ira directs Jack to a small room. Tony welcomes Nina and takes her into a secure room with no cameras. He is briefed on Kim and Teri and they decide to alert the Secret Service.

7:36 A.M. Jonathan joins Jack. Jonathan puts on latex fingerprint patches and orders Jack to assemble the gun in the briefcase. Desperate, Jack pulls a gun but is warned his family will die. Jack lets him leave.

7:41 A.M. Nina and Tony set a trap for Jamey. Tony pulls her out of the stall in between surveillance camera loops so Ira doesn't see and drags her into their safe room.

7:44 A.M. The Secret Service warns Palmer of the threat, but he proceeds. Security is ordered to bring in Bauer. Jamey refuses to talk without a lawyer.

7:52 A.M. An agent spots Jack. Palmer is moved from the podium safely. The sniper's plan is foiled. Tony and Nina get Jamey to message Ira. Ira gets a call from someone else and explains he has a backup plan. As Eli is about to kill Teri and Kim, Ira orders him to keep them alive.

7:59 A.M. The Secret Service takes Jack into custody.

The sniper takes aim.

Palmer is rushed off the stage.

Teri and Kim are close to death.

Actor Carlos Bernard says when he first came in to audition for *24*, the character was nothing like what eventually became Tony Almeida. "When I read the pilot script, before I actually auditioned for the role, he was very much a corporate backbiter and his name was Andrew Gellar. Andrew Gellar was a Jewish guy and I remember telling my agent it was an interesting script and I would go read for it, but I would never get it. I went into the audition and decided to do what I was going to do with it and *not* go with the way it was on the page — and they cast me."

During the first half of the season, Tony was portrayed as a very ambiguous character, willing to undermine Jack Bauer whenever he didn't perform procedures by the book. Bernard says the goal was to keep the audience guessing about the

character's true motivations. "I didn't know if he was going to end up as a bad guy or not. It was a whole different way to work when we started off the show. We didn't know what was going to happen and the director, Stephen Hopkins, had a way of using multiple cameras and one with a long lens that would catch everything you did. My take on it was that my character didn't trust anyone else and a lot of the time, if you are caught in a position of not trusting other people, you come off looking suspicious yourself. We did make a concerted effort not to play him as a straight up bad guy and to let the audience run with whatever they caught on to, and use their imaginations. I really played him as though he was a good guy and was the only one doing his job properly, and that, in turn, made him look suspicious, I think. There was also an adversarial relationship with Jack at that point. Tony still thought there was something going on between Nina and Jack, so there was this whole circle of distrust going on, and that added to the cloud of suspicion around the character. Myself, I always thought that Tony would end up being good because it was too obvious if he turned out to be a bad guy."

Research Files

PDA: Jamey uses a personal digital assistant (or PDA) to communicate remotely with Ira Gaines from the CTU women's bathroom. PDAs are popular handheld devices that have evolved from simple personal scheduling organizers into electronic hubs that can provide users with wireless access to the Internet, personal e-mail accounts, music libraries and even complete home computing systems. The first PC compatible palmtop was the Atari Portfolio in 1989. In 1996, Motorola released the PageWriter 2000, which the National Museum of American History selected for inclusion in its permanent collections as the first two-way text-messaging device. John Sculley coined the term 'PDA' in 1992 at the Consumer Electronics Show, when he was referring to the portable Apple Newton.

Additional Intel

Carlos Bernard reveals that he and Joel Surnow decided to change his character's name ten minutes before his first scene was shot for the pilot. Surnow came up with Tonio Almeida, short for Antonio, which Carlos didn't like. During the first scene, Kiefer couldn't say Tonio, and just called him Tony — the name stuck.

8:00 am - 9:00 am

Director: Stephen Hopkins
Writer: Virgil Williams

Guest Cast: Vicellous Reon Shannon (Keith Palmer), Devika Parikh (Maureen Kingsley), Michael Bryan French (Frank Simes)

"I used to be in the military. Did field work for the CIA. I've been to some horrible places, seen some horrible things... I don't think I've ever been this scared in my whole life." Jack Bauer

Timeframe

8:00 A.M. Palmer and Sherry leave the breakfast. Jack explains he was working to protect Palmer and the assassin is still at large. Jamey admits setting up the cameras for Ira Gaines. Jamey agrees to call Ira and calm him down about Jack. Milo is put on Jamey's projects.

8:09 A.M. Jack reveals the kidnapping of his family, but the Secret Service can't release him.

8:16 A.M. Despite his handcuffs, Jack acquires a gun, escapes and carjacks a waitress named Lauren to drive him away. They break into a construction site office to hide.

8:18 A.M. Jamey admits she got $300,000 from Ira. She wants immunity to talk more. Jack calls Nina and apologizes for shooting her. Jack is told about Jamey. Jack instructs Nina to bring Jamey's son to CTU, and to send him a car.

8:29 A.M. Sherry wants Palmer to fight the Maureen story.

8:31 A.M. Jack calls Tony and they both apologize. Lauren uses bolt cutters to take off Jack's handcuffs. Mike Novick tells Palmer about Jack Bauer. At the shed, Gaines' henchman Eli intends to rape Kim, but Teri offers herself instead.

8:40 A.M. Sherry persuades Maureen to hold the story on Keith for a few days in exchange for details about the breakfast attack.

8:44 A.M. Kim is hysterical, but Teri is strong and she steals Eli's phone. They call Nina, but have to hang up. Jack waits for his car with Lauren.

8:53 A.M. Tony and Nina threaten to tell Jamey's son. They leave her to think. Jack asks Lauren to get his car, but she runs to the police instead. Jack barely escapes.

8:57 A.M. Tony and Nina return to find Jamey in a pool of blood, having slit her wrist. Jamey's PDA rings with a call from Ira.

Key Events

Jack escapes and carjacks a waitress.

Teri sacrifices herself for Kim.

Nina and Tony find Jamey bleeding to death.

Joel Surnow details that, around the mid-point of season one, the writing staff were stuck figuring out where the last half of the season was going to go — especially the resolution of the mole arc. The storyline that Jamey Farrell was working as a mole for Ira Gaines could have just ended with her character's apparent suicide. But Surnow says they wanted that storyline to twist again to make an even bigger impact, which in turn led them to make Nina Myers the real mole.

"We set up the mole idea early in the season and, at the time, we didn't know who the heck the mole was," Surnow laughs. "We figured we would get to it later. Around episodes fourteen or fifteen, we realized we would have to reprise it as we came to the end of the season. At first we thought it couldn't be Nina because we already did a story where we sort of

exonerated her, so it had to be one of these three other people. Then we thought, 'What if it is Nina and she was the one that did that?' and then we added the whole story-line of her killing Jamey Farrell — which even caught us by surprise. If it surprises us, then the audience can't be that far ahead of it — and that's why we don't plot too much ahead. If you plot ahead, you sort of subconsciously give away the secret. That's why we never tell any of our actors their story arcs. We never told Sarah Clarke that she was bad. She just played the good, supportive, stable mate of Jack Bauer. If we had told her that she was bad, she would have had to do all that work in her head to get back to the thing that she was doing naturally."

Research Files

US Secret Service: The Secret Service contingent protecting Senator David Palmer remands Jack to the authority of the FBI for further investigation. The US Secret Service was commissioned on 5 July 1865 in Washington DC as a federal law enforcement agency under the US Department of Treasury until 2003, when it became part of the US Department of Homeland Security. The Secret Service's primary functions are to prevent the counterfeiting of US currency, investigate persons perpetrating fraud against the government, and to protect the President, Vice President, their families and any other high-ranking officials or visiting heads of state. The Secret Service has over 5,000 employees.

Additional Intel

Actress Kathleen Wilhoite plays the waitress, Lauren Proctor, who Jack carjacks and holds hostage in an office. The familiar character actress has appeared on more than fifty television series including recurring roles on *E.R.*, *Gilmore Girls*, *Mad About You* and *L.A. Law*.

9:00 am - 10:00 am

Director: Davis Guggenheim
Writer: Lawrence Hertzog

Guest Cast: Tamara Tunie (Alberta Green), Zeljko Ivanek (Andre Drazen), Daniel Bess (Rick), Currie Graham (Ted Cofell), Ivar Brogger (Frank Ames)

"I know most of you have been up more than twenty-four hours. Too bad. Nobody so much as yawns until we complete our objectives. If anybody has a problem with that, now would be a good time to resign." Alberta Green

Timeframe — Key Events

9:00 A.M. Medics work on Jamey and Nina informs CTU. Jack calls Nina for police roadblock help, while Teri calls Nina again. Nina connects them, but Teri has to hide her phone when Eli and Rick come back. Jack listens, while Milo tries to trace their location.

9:09 A.M. The Palmers continue to argue over Keith. Tony finds an encrypted file on Jamey's computer and gives it to Milo to crack. CTU gets the call — Jamey is dead.

9:18 A.M. Teri provides info about where they are being held. Milo needs twenty minutes to trace Teri's call. Jack evades police in a parking lot. Under a truck, he has a heartfelt talk with Teri and Kim. Eli returns, attacks Kim and the cell phone battery beeps. Eli hangs it up. The trace is broken.

9:32 A.M. Jack hotwires a car and escapes. Tony tells Jack that Jamey's file held the name Ted Cofell. Jack heads to Cofell's office. Andre Drazen calls Ira very upset and threatens to take the job away from him, as "this is personal".

9:36 A.M. Sherry calls Carl for help with Maureen. He admits he "took care" of the evidence. Jamey's e-mail shows a $1 million wire transfer to Ira from a Swiss bank account. They surmise Cofell did the transfer.

9:43 A.M. Tony informs Nina that Alberta Green is being sent as a provisional replacement for Jack at CTU.

9:46 A.M. Green arrives and tells CTU that Jack is a fugitive and their first priority. Palmer gets a call from a major supporter saying he knows about Keith through Carl and is backing out of the Palmer campaign. David is furious.

9:56 A.M. Nina lies to Green about speaking to Jack.

9:57 A.M. Cofell gets in his limo and doesn't notice Jack is at the wheel.

9:59 A.M. Kim sees her mom in pain, but Teri says it's nothing.

Jack and Teri finally talk again.

Alberta Green takes over CTU.

Jack takes command of Cofell's limo.

Right from the first season, *24* has always asked audiences to suspend disbelief regarding many aspects of the show. Be it the amount of time it takes to get from one part of Los Angeles to another without traffic, the scale of the current jeopardy, or just the abilities the characters have to navigate themselves out of impossible danger, audiences are willing to accept a lot within the *24* story format. Kiefer Sutherland says he is always aware of that unspoken agreement between the creative team and their audience. "From an actor's perspective, there is a very odd kind of understanding that exists with the audience that we have, the audience we've had from the beginning, that we're going to require them to take a bit of a leap of faith — not a bit of a leap actually, quite a big leap of faith — with us, and they have done that. This is one of those

circumstances where a show hit at the right time, at the right place, and the right audience. Whether that audience would have taken the leap of faith ten years ago or ten years from now, I don't know. But at that specific moment, they certainly were prepared to do that with us, and we rely on that from them. We've just been very fortunate to have people — an audience — who are open to doing that with us, to trying something new. The first season, it was amazing that people stuck with us the way they did. We were learning so much and at such an amazing pace and some stuff worked and some stuff didn't. They rode it out with us."

Research Files

Wireless Tracing: Teri Bauer leaves Eli's stolen cell phone on, allowing Milo and Nina to attempt to trace her location. In real life, cell phones can now be tracked to within a distance of fifty meters. In 2001, the Federal Communications Commission (FCC) ordered wireless service providers to be able to deliver the cell phone user's number and cell-site location information to a public safety agency. A cell phone's current position can be calculated by measuring the signal strength at a minimum of three cell base stations (low-powered, multi-channel, two-way radios which are in fixed locations), using triangulation to calculate the approximate position of the user. Soon, GPS (Global Positioning System) technology will become another tracking alternative to be implanted in cell phones. The emergent IEEE 802.11 wireless LAN (Local Area Network) technology is also fast becoming another viable tracking option.

Additional Intel

Actor Eric Balfour (Milo) was also working on episodes of the series *Six Feet Under* when he was shooting *24*. A potential haircut for his *SFU* character almost caused a continuity problem for *24* until producers on both shows worked out a compromise.

10:00 am - 11:00 am

Director: Davis Guggenheim
Writer: Robert Cochran

Guest Cast: Tamara Tunie (Alberta Green), Zeljko Ivanek (Andre Drazen), Richard Burgi (Kevin Carroll) Daniel Bess (Rick), Jude Ciccolella (Mike Novick)

"That's just it mom, I don't feel bad at all. I don't feel anything except happy he's dead." Kim Bauer

Timeframe	Key Events

10:00 A.M. Green alerts CTU that Belkin is a suspect in the Palmer assassination attempt. Jack locks Cofell in the car. He draws his gun, but Cofell says he knows nothing. Nina puts a file together on Cofell for Jack.

10:07 A.M. Rick returns to the shed, but he quickly leaves. Eli beats him. Tony diverts Green while Nina tells Jack about Cofell.

10:13 A.M. Jack threatens to torture Cofell, but he only admits he was meeting a businessman named Kevin Carroll. Jack drives him to the rendezvous.

10:20 A.M. Andre Drazen appears at Ira's compound and gives him thirty minutes to find Jack or he will pull the plug and kill Teri and Kim. Rick hears it all. Palmer orders Carl to meet him to talk.

10:30 A.M. Sherry and David fight about Carl. Novick informs Palmer more about Jack. Palmer asks about a mission two years ago, and Novick is surprised.

10:34 A.M. Jack and Cofell wait for Kevin. Cofell attacks Jack with a HALO knife. Jack overpowers him. Cofell curses at him in Serbian and suffers a heart attack. Desperate, Jack tries to feed him pills, but Cofell dies.

10:41 A.M. Nina tells Jack she thinks the Cofell connection is with Operation Nightfall.

10:44 A.M. Teri keeps Kim awake so they can run. Rick returns with a gun for Teri. Kevin arrives at the garage, gets in the back of the limo and tries to shoot Jack, but the partition is bulletproof.

10:51 A.M. Jack beats Kevin, who offers to take Jack to his family. The half-hour over, Drazen tells Ira to kill the women. Palmer talks to Carl and leaves an urgent message on George Ferragamo's answering machine.

10:59 A.M. Eli goes to kill Teri and Kim. Teri shoots but the gun is empty. Eli and Teri fight, she grabs his gun and shoots — twice, so Ira thinks Eli did his job.

Kevin shoots at Jack in the limo...

... but the glass partition is bulletproof.

Teri shoots Eli.

The first season of *24* established the overall balance of the series, relying on a mixture of permanent set shooting and a wide-range of location shoots all over the greater Los Angeles region. Location manager K.C. Warnke started on the show during the pilot and admits the first year was a pressure cooker for him and his key locations team. "The first season was really hard for a lot of different reasons. First of all, the network was heavily scrutinizing the writing, so it was constantly changing. Secondly, the crew was just getting to know one another and learning to work together. Plus, on the first season, there was a feeling of desperation all the time." Yoshi Enoki, of key locations, adds, "Because it's the first season, that's the season when you are going to establish the look, the feel, the tempo and everything, so I think there is a lot more pressure."

"The whole season you do feel like everything you do is under the microscope," Warnke continues. "Like, this could be the great scene that the network sees and loves; or this location has all these explosions; or this show has to get good ratings. There were also budget constraints on the first season, because no one wanted to spend a lot of money. So I would say the first season of *24*, for me, was the most difficult just because of those things." Enoki agrees saying, "Everybody has their reputations on the line, including the producers and the actors. Plus, if you set yourself up and you do something so explosive and exciting in the first season, you have to keep it going." Warnke adds enthusiastically, "I think we do the biggest stuff of any TV show in town. I can't think of any other show that does more as far as location work is concerned than we do; in terms of the action, the use of helicopters and the way we are always pushing the envelope."

Research Files

Microtech HALO: Ted Cofell whips out a very sophisticated Microtech HALO knife to attack Jack, which immediately blows his 'quiet businessman' cover. The Microtech HALO (High Altitude Low Opening) is widely considered the Cadillac of 'out the front' (or OTF) automatic opening knives. The HALO II has a four-inch ATS-34 blade that can be closed by pulling back on the recharging handle to re-cock the blade for its next use. The HALO II is not only a collectible item, but is considered a highly functional, all-purpose knife. The HALO knife was first produced in 1994, with three subsequent versions released since. The newest, HALO III, features a Tanto blade with no blade cutouts, an improved horizontal and vertical grip, and a more sturdy, slip-free firing button.

Additional Intel

During the fifteen-day production cycle of a *24* episode, the crew shoots at an average of four or five locations in the greater Los Angeles area. Over the 100-plus episodes of the series, that comes to more than 500 locations being featured on the show.

11:00 am - 12:00 pm

Director: Stephen Hopkins
Writer: Howard Gordon

Guest Cast: Michael Massee (Ira Gaines), Daniel Bess (Rick), Jude Ciccolella (Mike Novick), John Prosky (Dr. George Ferragamo)

"Alberta, you may have my office, but if you want to do my job, listen up." Jack Bauer

Timeframe   Key Events

11:00 A.M. Jack ties up Kevin and they drive to the compound where Teri and Kim are being held. Green ratchets up the search for Jack.

11:05 A.M. Teri and Kim hide Eli's body under a tub, take his knife and cover the blood. Nina sends satellite images of Ira's compound to Jack. She begs him to call Green so they can send backup, but Jack says no. He puts Kevin in the driver's seat and they enter the gate.

11:09 A.M. Palmer tells Novick about Carl's plan to silence the therapist. Novick is livid Palmer called Ferragamo. Kevin tries to psyche out Jack, but Jack ignores him then knocks him out.

11:16 A.M. Ira clears out his control room and Jack hides from the armed guards.

11:20 A.M. Palmer talks to Ferragamo, but the therapist thinks Palmer is threatening him. Teri and Kim are reunited with Jack.

11:28 A.M. Green suspects Nina and Tony are in contact with Jack so she suspends them.

11:30 A.M. Rick enters the shed and Jack goes to strangle him, but Kim and Teri defend him. Rick offers one of Ira's vans to help them all escape. Green interrogates Tony.

11:39 A.M. Rick is intercepted at the van by Ira, who orders Rick to take him to the unconscious body of Kevin Carroll.

11:42 A.M. Novick briefs Palmer on Ferragamo, but when they arrive at his office, it's engulfed in flames and the therapist is dead. They drive away. Green is about to fire Tony, when Jack calls with the coordinates of the hideout.

11:52 A.M. Green retracts Nina and Tony's suspension.

11:54 A.M. Gaines revives Kevin and Rick steals a van, picks up the Bauers, and a shootout occurs. Jack sends Teri and Kim off with his map, while he and Rick stay. A bullet clips Rick and Jack fires at the gas tank making the van explode.

11:59 A.M. Jack helps Rick escape.

Jack, Teri and Kim reunite.

Ferragamo dies in a suspicious fire.

Jack blows up Ira's van.

Amazingly enough, one of the most expensive pieces of clothing ever created and used on *24* was for the character of Ira Gaines' lackey and Kim's crush, Rick (Daniel Bess). The item in question was the average-looking flannel shirt that he wears in the pilot and continues to have on throughout the course of the season. Costume designer Jim Lapidus details, "When they did the pilot, Rick had a vintage plaid shirt on. There was one from the shoot and I found another one, so we had two of them. As the season progressed, they decided they were going to shoot him in the arm, so there was going to be blood and they were going to use a stunt double. So Jean took the sleeves of the flannel shirt and talked to the silk screening people." Costume supervisor Jean Rosone continues, "They took photographs of the plaid from the vintage shirt and isolated it, so they could

duplicate it. They made panels — when that happens, you pay per square inch. Then we took the shirts to the garment maker, who drew out the pieces. Then it had to go back to the people who printed the plaid because the plaid had to be in the right place, like with the pockets in the same place." Lapidus adds, "And then once it was put together, it had to be aged down to look as old as the one he was wearing." Sighing. Rosone reveals, "By the time we got done, we had made three shirts to shoot and they were $1,000 apiece."

Research Files

Global Positioning System: Jack asks Nina to GPS his location through his Palm Pilot, so he can view satellite images of the area where Teri and Kim are being held. GPS is a satellite network originally designed for the US military and funded by the US Department of Defense. With hand-held consumer receivers, anyone can now track their latitude, longitude, altitude and velocity. The satellite system (which consists of twenty-four satellites orbiting the Earth every twelve hours) is maintained at the Master Control facility at Schriever Air Force Base (formerly Falcon AFB) in Colorado. Due to its impressive accuracy, the GPS system has drawn fire from security organizations concerned that the technology could be used for criminal activity, so the Pentagon initiated selective availability, in which the most accurate signals (pinpointing positions down to a few feet) would be reserved strictly for military use, while others would get readings accurate to 100 feet.

Additional Intel

For the first three years of production, the permanent sets for *24*, including the CTU compound, were located in Woodland Hills, California.

Teri Bauer

Experience:

Graphic Eye – Partner and Head Designer
Click California Design – Creative Director
LA Design – Graphic Artist
Chiat/Day Advertising – Graphic Artist
Museum of Contemporary Art, Los Angeles –
 Installation Assistant Curator
Los Angeles County Museum – Consultant to the Director
Santa Monica Gallery – Assistant to the Director
Greenpeace Organization – Advertising Art Director
Dark Horse Comics – Colorist
Isabella Gardner Museum (Boston) – Art Conservator
Uffizi Galleria (Florence, Italy) – Restorative Assistant

Education:

University of California (Berkeley) – Master of Fine Arts,
 Art Practice
Rhode Island School of Design – Bachelor of Arts, Painting

Personal:

Married – Jack Bauer
Daughter – Kimberly Bauer

David Palmer

Experience:

United States Congress – Senator (MD)
Senate Appropriations Committee – Member
Senate Commerce Subcommittee – Member
United States Congress, Representative (MD)
House Ethics Committee – Chairman
House Ways and Means Committee – Member
House National Security Subcommittee – Member
Maryland State Congress – Representative (Baltimore)
Fidley, Barrow & Bain – Attorney at Law

Education:

University of Maryland School of Law – Juris Doctorate
Georgetown University – Bachelor of Arts, Political Economy

Honors:

NCAA All-American – Men's Basketball
Big East Conference – Defensive Player of the Year
Sporting News – College Player of the Year
Wooden Award for Player of the Year

Personal:

Married – Sherry Palmer
Son – Keith Palmer
Daughter – Nicole Palmer

12:00 pm - 1:00 pm

Director: Stephen Hopkins
Writer: Andrea Newman

Guest Cast: Michael Massee (Ira Gaines), Tamara Tunie (Alberta Green), Daniel Bess (Rick), Zeljko Ivanek (Andre Drazen), Zach Grenier (Carl Webb)

"I'm running for President, Mike. I'm going to win." Senator Palmer

Timeframe	Key Events

12:00 P.M. Ira searches for the Bauers. Kim and Teri head for the water tower. Nina is worried she can't reach Jack. Novick and Palmer argue on what to do next about Maureen's story, so they consult Sherry. Ira tells Drazen what happened and the Serb orders him to deliver Jack's dead body.

12:10 P.M. Jack and Rick arrive at the tower, but Kim and Teri get lost in the woods.

12:16 P.M. Sherry agrees with Novick and says Palmer will have the power to go against Carl once he's in office.

12:20 P.M. Jack calls Green about going back for his family, and she sends reinforcements. Teri and Kim hide in an abandoned mine. A thug finds them, but Jack appears and rescues his family.

12:29 P.M. Tony and Nina interrogate Jamey's mother about the money deposited in her bank account. Palmer talks to Maureen and finds out she left her job because of threats from Carl's people.

12:35 P.M. Tony and Nina discover the transferred money in Jamey's account came from an account in Belgrade. Ira and Kevin find the Bauers and barrage Jack with gunfire. Jack blinds Ira and grazes him with a bullet. CTU's chopper arrives.

12:41 P.M. Palmer plans to confess to the DA, but Carl shows up and says he will plant evidence to link Keith to two murders. Palmer lets the DA leave.

12:51 P.M. Kim looks for Rick and Jack follows a trail of Gaines' blood. He finds Ira and asks about the Belgrade connection. Jack offers immunity, but Ira raises his gun and Jack kills him. Jack then boards the chopper with Teri and Kim, while Rick escapes on a bus.

12:59 P.M. Alberta Green learns from Nina and Tony that another assassin left Yugoslavia earlier in the morning and is already in Los Angeles.

Jack shoots Ira.

The Bauer family is rescued.

Alexis, the new assassin, arrives.

As the season progressed and more scenes were shot outside of CTU, the various production departments began to encounter a variety of challenges that arose as they moved outside of the controlled studio sets. During the raid on Ira Gaines' compound, it became apparent to the costume department that there were serious physical limitations surrounding Elisha Cuthbert's wardrobe. "From the pilot, Kim was in high-heel, platform, wedgie sandals, with open-toes and everything," costume designer Jim Lapidus remembers. "Elisha is five-foot-one, so the shoes gave her height. But then we got to the point in the season where we were shooting on a mountaintop and she had to run down the mountain. The guys came back from the location scout and told us there were gopher holes. They had worn hiking boots and said it was still really hard for them to walk around, and Kim was supposed to run around in her

Research Files

Belgrade: Nina Myers discovers that a second assassin was sent from Belgrade, Yugoslavia, to Los Angeles to kill Palmer. Belgrade is one of the oldest cities in Europe, being where the Celts settled in the third century BC. The city is the capital of both Serbia and the former Yugoslavia. Belgrade also has the status of a separate territorial unit in Serbia, with its own autonomous city government, divided into seventeen municipalities. It was an area of particular unrest in the late 1980s when the then-President of Serbia, Slobodan Milosevic, fanned the ethnic nationalism of Serbs, which led to a particularly brutal civil war between Croats, Muslims and Serbs that lasted until NATO launched air strikes on Kosovo on 24 March 1999. Milosevic was eventually ousted from power to stand trial for war crimes, but died in prison in 2006.

Additional Intel

Leslie Hope admits when they were in the helicopter and she was hugging Kiefer and whispering in his ear during the scene, she was making "off-color" comments in an attempt to crack him up. She also reveals that Elisha Cuthbert has a fear of helicopters so the girl they were clutching as Kim was actually a stand-in.

platform wedgies!" Costume supervisor Jean Rosone continues, "So I took a picture of her foot in the sandal, gave it to the set painter and said, 'This is what I need these shoes to look like.' He painted toes and a strap onto sneakers, and when she is running through the dirt during the episode, it worked." Cuthbert used those special painted shoes for the entire story arc on the mountain. Lapidus laughs, "Some of the fans noticed it, but all you need is for the actress to twist an ankle and she would have been out!"

1:00 pm - 2:00 pm

Director: Jon Cassar
Writers: Joel Surnow & Michael Loceff

Guest Cast: Tamara Tunie (Alberta Green), Misha Collins (Alexis Drazen), Paul Schulze (Ryan Chappelle), Kara Zediker (Elizabeth Nash)

"I'm not the biggest fan of Jack Bauer. I don't agree with the way he delegates authority and I don't like the way he runs operations, but since midnight last night, you won't get me to disapprove of a single action he's taken." Tony Almeida

Timeframe

1:00 P.M. The Bauers arrive at CTU. Kim and Teri are taken to the clinic and Jack begs Nina to watch over them.

1:07 P.M. Sherry tries once more to change Palmer's mind and is surprised when he agrees to remain silent. He explains Carl's threat and tells Sherry not to tell Keith. Teri asks the doctor not to tell Jack about the rape.

1:15 P.M. Keith overhears Palmer and Novick talking about Ferragamo and is upset. He wants to go public finally, but Palmer says no.

1:18 P.M. CTU Regional Director Ryan Chappelle arrives to interrogate Jack. At the clinic, Nina comes across an agent who she determines isn't official and she begins to question Teri and Kim's safety.

1:29 P.M. Chappelle debriefs Jack, and tells him he can't be reinstated. Jack contends he is valuable in protecting Palmer. Nina interrupts with a phone call, and she questions Jack about another possible mole.

1:33 P.M. Alexis, the shooter, arrives and detonates a bomb that destroys Ira's compound. He also shoots Kevin dead.

1:41 P.M. Tony recommends that Palmer leave California. Green offers Tony a promotion if he'll turn on Jack.

1:42 P.M. Green debriefs Jack and doesn't allow him to call his family. Jack says they need the CIA Balkan terrorist database to figure out the Cofell connection. Sherry stops Keith from telling the police his story. Palmer says they need to pack up for Nevada due to the threat on his life.

1:51 P.M. Nina gets permission to transfer Teri and Kim to a safe house. Tony supports Jack. Novick tells Palmer he thinks Jack is bent on revenge. Meanwhile, Palmer's aide, Elizabeth Nash, is having an affair with Alexis.

1:59 P.M. Palmer arrives at CTU to speak with Jack.

Key Events

Ryan Chappelle interrogates Jack.

Kevin is killed by Alexis.

Senator Palmer arrives at CTU.

After spending half the season orbiting each other's lives, Senator Palmer finally took it into his own hands to confront Jack Bauer face-to-face at CTU. It became one of the most powerful moments of the first season, watching these two larger-than-life men inhabit the same space. Executive producer Howard Gordon enthuses, "It was a great moment. We loved it and the two of them played so well together. We hoped their paths would cross, but it was a matter of where these two characters were. Obviously, Palmer was more static and Jack was bouncing all over Los Angeles and, at various points, was assigned to kill him by the bad guys. Now, here are these two guys whose destinies are entwined, who are thrown together, and this was the basis of so much of the show — the relationship between Jack and David Palmer. The chemistry between them really fulfilled the promise of that relationship. I thought

they were great together. They haven't crossed paths very many times during the course of the show, so what's amazing is that their relationship is quite profound. I love the expression on Kiefer's face of respect and admiration and the respect and admiration David Palmer felt in return — those feelings were beautifully communicated by both of them." The intensity of that first meeting worked so well it helped inspire the writers to create future connections in subsequent seasons. "It absolutely did," Gordon details. "When you think about that relationship, we think we played it to a bust. We tried to keep David Palmer in the show as long as our imaginations allowed."

Research Files

Langley: Jack tells Alberta Green to get in contact with Langley and to have them open up their database on Balkan terrorists. Langley, Virginia, is the main operating location of the Central Intelligence Agency (CIA). The agency was created in 1947 by President Harry S. Truman to obtain and analyze information about foreign governments, business entities, and individuals who pose a threat to the United States, and disseminate the information to the various branches of the U.S. Government. The CIA seal looks like a compass, with sixteen points representing the agency's search for data all over the world; and it rests on a shield, which represents the agency's protection of the United States.

Additional Intel

The first season of *24* occurs on the day of the fictional California Presidential Primary. This episode first aired on 5 March 2002, the actual day of the real California Presidential Primary.

2:00 pm - 3:00 pm

Director: Jon Cassar
Writer: Michael Chernuchin

Guest Cast: Tamara Tunie (Alberta Green), Zeljko Ivanek (Andre Drazen), Daniel Bess (Rick), Wade Williams (Robert Ellis), Misha Collins (Alexis Drazen)

"What's incredible is that this has nothing to do with me running for President. It has nothing to do with my being black. It's just revenge for taking out Victor Drazen." Senator Palmer

Timeframe — Key Events

2:00 P.M. Chappelle orders Palmer kept away from Jack. Milo confirms the name of the third shooter is Alexis Drazen.

2:04 P.M. Nina explains to Kim and Teri they are going to a safe house. Kim asks about her mom's pains and Teri explains it's an ovarian cyst. Green continues to grill Jack but he refuses to talk until he gets his call. Elizabeth tells Alexis that she and Palmer are going to Nevada.

2:07 P.M. Palmer calls a Defense Department official to get in to see Jack. Palmer accuses Jack of wanting revenge for Operation Nightfall. Jack denies the allegation and explains his side.

2:16 P.M. Teri takes a home pregnancy test. Palmer and Jack work out their connections and realize today is the two-year anniversary of when they took out Victor Drazen. They also realize the third operative of the mission, Robert Ellis, must be in danger too and they call him immediately.

2:21 P.M. Teri's test is positive.

2:24 P.M. Elizabeth calls Alexis to update him. Alexis assures his brother, Andre, that Palmer will be dead by midnight.

2:31 P.M. Teri tries to call Jack to no avail. Kim swipes Nina's cell phone to call Rick. Palmer is shocked the threat to his life is about revenge.

2:43 P.M. A report from Ellis reveals Drazen's wife and daughter were killed in Operation Nightfall. Palmer orders Chappelle to step up protection on Teri and Kim. Nina and Teri talk and it comes out that Jack and Nina were lovers.

2:53 P.M. Palmer orders Jack be reinstated. Palmer apologizes to Jack. More security is sent to the safe house. Teri doesn't get a chance to tell Jack about the baby.

2:59 P.M. Jack and Ellis talk on the phone about a missing file, when someone comes in and chokes Ellis to death.

Jack and Palmer meet face-to-face.

Teri's pregnancy test is positive.

Teri and Nina talk.

One of the more low-key, but incredibly important confrontations of the season was the conversation at the safe house between Nina and Teri. Previously friendly with one another, their conversation quickly goes downhill when it comes out that Nina had an affair with Jack during the Bauer separation. The subsequent tense tête-à-tête between the women became a favorite scene for the actresses. Sarah Clarke says, "We were very proud of that scene and really happy that the producers realized that it was necessary." Leslie Hope concurs, "It was one of my favorite scenes, so watching Sarah play the scene, and what she did with it, was so good!"

Clarke details that they were able to get the producers to allow them to tweak the scene together, to make it more genuine from a female perspective. "They were really great with our input about how women talk. A lot of the time, you get scenes like this

and even if they set up the scenario right, the dialogue between the women just isn't right. I think the thing we hit upon is that women usually know what the other person is going to say. Women have great instincts and intuition and usually they just want to hear the other say out loud what they already know. So when we read the first couple of drafts, it was just way over-spoken. [Director] Jon Cassar was really great in whittling it down with us. It was all about what was *not* said, and that worked really well for us. It was exciting."

Research Files

Operation Nightfall: Jack and Palmer discuss their joint connection to the failed mission that occurred in Kosovo and sparked the current day's situation. Operation Nightfall was led by then-Captain Jack Bauer of the US Army's 1st Special Forces Operational Detachment-Delta (commonly known as the Delta Force). The mission, which was not sanctioned by NATO, was approved by Senator Palmer and organized by NSA agent Robert Ellis to take out the ethnic-cleansing war criminal Victor Drazen. Jack thought they killed Drazen, but later learned it was a double, though Drazen's wife and daughter were killed. At the end of the mission, Serbian forces ambushed the team and everyone except Jack perished. Jack left the military and joined CTU.

Additional Intel

The four songs featured in this episode are 'I'm on the Wonder' by Clifton Chenier, 'I'm a Doggy' by Marvin Pontiac, 'Clocks Grow Old' by I Am Spoonbender and 'Louisiana Two-Step' by Clifton Chenier.

3:00 pm - 4:00 pm

Director: Stephen Hopkins
Writers: Robert Cochran & Howard Gordon

Guest Cast: Zeljko Ivanek (Andre Drazen), Xander Berkeley (George Mason), Navi Rawat (Melanie), Henri Lubatti (Jovan Myovic)

> "Things tend to get complicated when you screw your boss." Teri Bauer

Timeframe — Key Events

3:00 P.M. Milo briefs Jack on the three possible shooters. Elizabeth calls her lover, Alexis, and they agree to meet at 4:30 P.M.

3:05 P.M. Jack gets an odd vibe from Teri. Milo forwards pictures of the possible assassins to the Palmer campaign and Elizabeth recognizes Alexis. Nina becomes concerned talking to Kim that she has feelings for Rick.

3:11 P.M. Palmer alerts Jack to Elizabeth's affair with Alexis. They send a chopper for her and Jack tells Palmer he assumes Ellis is dead. Kim calls Rick again. Meanwhile, Teri and Nina's debrief is going poorly and Nina suggests someone else finishes it.

3:20 P.M. Palmer talks to Keith and promises to be a better father, but Keith is upset when he's told they are holding back on the Ferragamo story. At the safe house, assassin Jovan Myovic takes out the CTU agents outside.

3:28 P.M. Jack's clearance is downgraded, but Milo gets him into the system. An angry Keith arranges to meet Carl at Griffith Observatory. Myovic enters the safe house.

3:41 P.M. A CTU agent puts Teri and Kim in a closet for safety. Two shooters ambush the agent, but Teri and Kim escape with a car from the garage. Nina arrives back at CTU and Jack is surprised.

3:46 P.M. Myovic chases Kim and Teri. She loses him, pulls over and gets out. When the verge gives way, the car slides down a cliff and explodes. Teri thinks Kim is dead and passes out.

3:52 P.M. Keith and Carl meet and the two men throw threats at one another. Carl intends to make sure Keith is framed for murder and leaves. Keith takes out a tape recorder that recorded the entire conversation.

3:55 P.M. Myovic gives up the search. Teri wakes up with amnesia and is offered a ride by a woman.

3:59 P.M. Kim wakes up bruised, but fine.

Teri watches the car with Kim in it explode.

Keith and Carl square off.

Kim wakes up alive.

Being a Bauer woman is not an easy job on *24*. Leslie Hope and Elisha Cuthbert reveal they took comfort in overcoming the challenges the season threw at them by bonding during the especially stressful times. In particular, they cite the arc that had them locked in a shed at the Gaines compound. "Some of the hardest scenes in season one, I think, were doing a lot of the stuff in the barn with Leslie Hope," Cuthbert details. "I remember vividly being stuck in there and filming in that environment for almost a month and a half. It just went on and on and was sort of grueling; we were stuck there wondering where the characters were going to go. I don't think I realized how intense the show was going to be until it came out. At the time, when you are shooting it, you aren't worried about whether people are going to see it. You are just there getting it done and trying to make every scene great."

For Hope, the entire season was a test of resilience and focus. "I never had anyone come visit me on set. As much as I loved being there, I really had to go to work. I never felt like I was just mucking about and that it would be easy. I think that's what made the cast such a tight group because it felt like we were all together, helping each other through it."

Cuthbert says the familial bond between the actors translated to the Bauer family as well. "The funny thing about Kim is that Jack can be running around in this crazy action-packed show all day long, but when he comes back to his wife and child, you see him go into a real place. These are the two people he cares about and it made him real, I think. It brings him down to Earth and it's great to see that change from hero to real man."

Research Files

Griffith Observatory: Carl asks Keith Palmer to meet him at Griffith Park Observatory to discuss George Ferragamo's death and the murder cover-up. Griffith Observatory is a legendary landmark and space observatory located on Mount Hollywood in LA's Griffith Park. Colonel Griffith J. Griffith donated the land to the City of Los Angeles in 1896, and the observatory officially opened on 14 May 1935. Boasting a fantastic view of Los Angeles, the observatory features exhibits about astronomy and other space-related topics. The site is also a big attraction for movie lovers, having been featured in such films as *Bowfinger*, *The Terminator* and, perhaps most famously, *Rebel Without a Cause*.

Additional Intel

Actor Carlos Bernard does not appear in this episode, but Tony Almeida is featured in every subsequent episode of the next three seasons.

4:00 pm - 5:00 pm

Director: Stephen Hopkins
Writer: Michael Chernuchin

Guest Cast: Zeljko Ivanek (Andre Drazen), Vicellous Reon Shannon (Keith Palmer), Vincent Angell (Dr. Phil Parslow), Daniel Bess (Rick)

> "Sir, this has nothing to do with payback. This is simply the best way to nail these guys, period."
> Jack Bauer

Timeframe

4:00 P.M. Kim roams the hillside looking for her mother. Jack brings Elizabeth back to Palmer's hotel for a meeting with Alexis.

4:05 P.M. Teri asks to be let off at a restaurant she remembers. Elizabeth agrees to bring down Alexis, despite Palmer's protest. Jack thinks it's the best plan.

4:15 P.M. Kim calls CTU from a payphone and talks to Tony. She says the safe house agents are dead and she won't talk to anyone but Nina or her dad and hangs up.

4:17 P.M. Tony sends a team to the safe house and wants to call Jack, but Mason tells him Jack needs to focus on Alexis and Elizabeth. Nina is concerned about Jack's judgment. Desperate, Kim calls Rick and threatens him unless he helps her.

4:22 P.M. Keith returns, apologizes to his dad and plays back the tape with Carl on it. Palmer asks for Keith's trust and takes the tape.

4:27 P.M. Andre orders Alexis to kill Elizabeth when he is done getting information from her. Jack assures Elizabeth she is secure and will be watched by an entire team.

4:31 P.M. Teri meets the manager of the restaurant and he offers to call her friend Dr. Parslow to come assist her.

4:32 P.M. Jack finds out from Nina that Teri knows about their affair. Before more can be said, Alexis arrives and the plan is in action.

4:39 P.M. Elizabeth manages to plant a transmitter in Alexis' wallet, but then she plunges a letter opener into his stomach. SWAT enters the room to keep Alexis alive.

4:55 P.M. Kim arrives at Rick's house and meets his angry girlfriend, Melanie.

4:57 P.M. Dr. Phil Parslow meets Teri at the restaurant.

4:59 P.M. Palmer and Mason are livid with Jack, but Alexis' cell phone rings and someone directs him to bring the money to a man in a red baseball hat at Connie's in Mid-Wilshire.

Key Events

Elizabeth stabs Alexis and Jack races in.

Kim meets Rick and his girlfriend.

Teri meets Dr. Parslow again.

After a season's worth of incredible stress and danger, Teri Bauer finally cracks when she thinks she witnesses the death of her daughter in a fiery car crash. Shocked, she passes out and awakens with amnesia. The storyline received a lot of negative feedback from critics and some fans, and even gave pause to Leslie Hope. "I was along for the *24* ride but the only time I was worried, not surprisingly, was when that first amnesia script came down the pike," she admits. "After the pilot, it became clear that we as actors would have to carry this emotional weight week after week for nine months. What became clear though, especially with Stephen Hopkins, who directed the pilot and many other episodes, was that I had become so confident in his ability to carry this long thread of emotion, drama and story point. It was sort of a relief that you always knew what your past and your present was, and you didn't have to reach that

far back to get to it. Having said that, as much grief as I got for the amnesia storyline, it was kind of a relief for me, about three or four months in, to dump all the emotional baggage and just start over."

Hope did present her concerns about the story arc and she laughs remembering the response. "I called up Stephen Hopkins and said, 'I'm a little worried about this whole amnesia thing.' Stephen very calmly replied, 'Well you should be.' It was the only time as an actor I wasn't sure if I could pull it off. Obviously, I wasn't writing the show, so I can't take any responsibility for the storyline, but I didn't know and I still don't honestly, how much better I could have done that or what more I could have brought to it. But every week they really gave me such great opportunities, particularly as the wife, so it was a big gift for me to be on the show."

Research Files

Fiber Optics: Jack explains to Elizabeth Nash that the room has been outfitted with tiny fiber optic cameras that will allow them to see every corner of the suite. Fiber optic technology is based upon clustering together long, thin strands of optical fibers (made of pure glass about the diameter of a human hair) to transmit light signals and data over long distances. The image resolution with fiber optics remains very high, without degradation, unlike standard long distance cable feeds, which can suffer from signal fade. Fiber optic cameras are used for covert surveillance due to their small size and weight. They are also perfect for keyhole surgery.

Additional Intel

Due to the intense continuity demands of the series, it's absolutely necessary for photos to be taken of every scene, set and character throughout the season to match the episodes. Prop master Sterling Rush averages ten to twelve thousand of those photos per season.

5:00 pm - 6:00 pm

Director: Frederick K. Keller
Writer: Maurice Hurley

Guest Cast: Zeljko Ivanek (Andre Drazen), Xander Berkeley (George Mason), Kirk Baltz (Teddy Hanlin), Eric Balfour (Milo Pressman)

> "I will do anything to protect my family, David. Anything. Does that make me a bad person?"
> Sherry Palmer

Timeframe — Key Events

5:00 P.M. Jack begs Palmer to keep his security at high alert. They find money in the hotel room and Jack plans to go to the drop off. Kim realizes Rick hasn't told anyone Dan is dead.

5:06 P.M. Dr. Parslow tells Teri about her life and that they were very close. He offers to take her to the hospital but she refuses. Palmer plays the Carl confession tape for Sherry and Mike Novick.

5:11 P.M. Jack calls Tony about his family. Mason lies and tells him they are both sleeping safely.

5:16 P.M. Tony wants more people trying to find Kim and Teri.

5:19 P.M. Andre Drazen calls Jovan Myovic looking for his brother, Alexis.

5:22 P.M. Rick and Melanie insist that Kim leave before Dan's brother, Frank, returns. Kim and Rick kiss goodbye, but Frank arrives before she can leave.

5:30 P.M. Nina and Jack set up security for the meeting, and learn a bitter agent named Teddy Hanlin is assigned as Jack's backup. Tony gets a report that a woman matching Teri's description was in a car accident.

5:32 P.M. Dr. Parslow doesn't find any signs of trauma on Teri and takes her home.

5:36 P.M. Sherry finds Keith's tape in the safe and destroys it. Palmer confronts her saying it was a test to see how far she would go. Palmer is furious and has Novick set up a press conference within the hour.

5:45 P.M. Hanlin starts to taunt Jack about their past. Nina calls Mason on Hanlin.

5:53 P.M. Myovic waits outside the Bauer house. Kim and Rick are concerned about Frank's intention to do a drug deal.

5:55 P.M. Jack meets the man in the cap and learns the plan is to shut off the power grid for five minutes at 7:30 P.M. The man runs. Hanlin takes a shot against orders and kills him.

5:59 P.M. Myovic sees Dr. Parslow and Teri arrive.

Kim and Rick kiss.

Palmer confronts Sherry about the tape.

Hanlin shoots the man in the cap.

As the Bauers were in constant turmoil throughout season one, so too was the Palmer family. From the pilot episode and Palmer's mysterious phone call, the foundation was laid for a storyline rife with intense revelations and drama. Executive producer Howard Gordon details the original concept, "When Joel and Bob wrote the pilot, in their minds, they had the idea of a story we were going to tell regarding Dennis Haybert's character and this unexplained death. His daughter had been raped and Palmer had actually, himself, killed the kid who date raped her."

Interestingly, Haysbert almost didn't get the role of Palmer: "Dennis was exactly who we wanted from the very beginning," Gordon reveals. "When he walked in to read for the part, he was really the only one we ever wanted. However, from what I understand, there was some resistance from the studio and the network who felt Dennis might not be a compelling enough

actor. Fortunately, whatever reservations they had obviously didn't hold for very long."

With Haysbert now cast, Gordon says his mere presence dictated changes in the original direction of the story. "For one thing, it was the wrong strategy regardless of which actor we chose, but Dennis was clearly the moral center of the show, so the murder was an action that really didn't fit his character. Dennis really had a profound effect on the way we told that story — where Palmer was the innocent. He was a guy who was discovering a secret that his family had collectively held from him. It was a fall from innocence, but he was such a righteous person that it was okay for him to be innocent and maybe even to be somewhat naïve. In some ways, this is really the first day where his innocence is lost and his ideals are compromised. It marked the beginning of the path that Palmer followed for the rest of his time on the show."

Research Files

Dissociative Amnesia: After the car explosion with Kim, Teri Bauer escapes death only to wake up not remembering the details of her life or the horrific day. Dissociative Amnesia occurs when a person suffers exposure to an extremely traumatic event. The person is unable to cope and literally dissociates themselves from a situation or experience too traumatic to integrate with their conscious self. This type of amnesia is not always contingent on some type of medical trauma, but is often triggered for a specific window of time, like the impact point of a car accident and its aftermath.

Additional Intel

Kiefer Sutherland won the Golden Globe Award for Best Performance by an Actor in a Television Series — Drama in 2002 for the first season of *24*.

Nina Myers

CONFIDENTIAL

To be used for Internal Investigation

Victor Drazen

Nationality:

Serbian

Experience:

Committed atrocities in Kosovo as a member of various violent paramilitary organisations.

Personal:

Wife – Vesna Drazen (deceased)
Daughter – Martina Drazen (deceased)
Sons – Alexis Drazen, Andre Drazen

6:00 pm - 7:00 pm

Director: Frederick K. Keller
Writers: Joel Surnow & Michael Loceff

Guest Cast: Zeljko Ivanek (Andre Drazen), Megalyn Echikunwoke (Nicole Palmer), Edoardo Ballerini (Frank Allard), Xander Berkeley (George Mason)

"Nice, Jack. Have you noticed how there's always a body count everywhere you go?"
George Mason

Timeframe — Key Events

6:00 P.M. Teri's house alarm goes off.

6:05 P.M. Nina reveals the dead man was set to turn the power off in one section of LA. Palmer calls Jack, he has found the missing Drazen file, and in it is an address in the city of Saugus. Tony confirms the city is within the blackout coordinates. Mason and Jack go to Saugus.

6:09 P.M. Frank is furious with Dan. Kim tries to escape and blurts out Dan isn't coming. Rick admits Dan is dead. Frank says it's too late to stop the drug deal.

6:15 P.M. The Palmer family argues over dinner, as Sherry questions whether her husband has the strength to become President.

6:18 P.M. Nina determines the Saugus address is a wildlife preserve.

6:28 P.M. Palmer says he wants his family's support at the press conference. Sherry says she won't argue.

6:30 P.M. Parslow greets his friend Chris, who brings a gun. Teri freaks out. Myovic tells Andre Drazen that Teri is now in the house.

6:33 P.M. At the press conference, Palmer admits everything. Carl watches in anger and vows to take care of it, but his cronies say it's too late.

6:40 P.M. At CTU, Nina learns of the missing Bauer women. She is livid with Tony and Mason, who won't let her talk to Jack.

6:43 P.M. Jack tells Mason about the Drazen connections and they come across a power transformer in the middle of the field.

6:46 P.M. Nina checks the local hospitals for Teri and Kim. The drug deal is a setup and SWAT enters to arrest everyone, including Kim.

6:55 P.M. Palmer finishes the press conference taking full responsibility for the entire affair and asks the voters to forgive him. Myovic enters the Bauer house and shoots both Chris and Parslow. Tony arrives and shoots Myovic. Teri's memory rushes back.

6:59 P.M. Mason and Jack reach the GPS address and a helicopter approaches.

Palmer confesses at the press conference.

Tony kills Myovic.

A helicopter finds Mason and Jack.

This episode marked the first time the characters of Jack Bauer and George Mason left CTU together as they jointly followed up a lead concerning the Drazens. The dramatic shot of the two men in an empty field with the sun setting behind them became a memorable moment for actor Xander Berkeley, who played Mason. "To me, there was a great liberation in just being out of the office," he smiles. "To suddenly be thrown out into a field, opened up the dynamics between Kiefer and I. We could do all kinds of things when we were out there to create a camaraderie, and yet a rivalry."

Remembering the day of the shoot, Berkeley says, "We didn't have enough time to do the final shot. I remember the whole group of us running out to that field to get that one last shot. The gaffers were running and people were running cable. There were other little elements too, like I had these really cool sunglasses

and then suddenly, as the sun was going down, the handheld camera guys said they were seeing the sun coming down in my sunglasses. The scene also crackles with the tension of the fact that you only have one shot to get this in, because the next time you try, the sun's gone — and we got it. It was one of those things where it's great when you can capture that moment on film. It was a great seasoned group of people who had been shooting and acting together that day, and we all pulled together. It was one of those times when we were a team and we beat the odds."

Having watched the episode, Berkeley says he was even more impressed with the finished shot. "The camera department situated themselves so, suddenly, I'm behind Kiefer and the composer put in some creepy music — the next thing you know the tension builds and I didn't have to do anything! I'm just hanging out with Kiefer," he laughs.

Research Files

SWAT Teams: A SWAT team bursts into the residence shared by Rick and Dan to arrest the inhabitants, including Kim Bauer. SWAT teams (or Special Weapons And Tactics) are specialized paramilitary police units trained to handle particularly dangerous situations where skills such as marksmanship, exposure to explosives, negotiations, K9 unit handling and hand-to-hand combat might be needed. The first SWAT unit was created in the city of Delano, California, during the 1960s, and teams are now operating in almost every major United States city police station. On average, the LAPD SWAT Team handles ninety barricaded suspect incidents and serves fifty high-risk warrants a year.

Additional Intel

Joel Surnow admits the writers use real-life inspiration to name characters. Surnow uses the names of tennis players; Cochran uses chess players; and producer Michael Loceff, also a teacher at Foothill College, uses people from the college. Also, many names come from charity auctions where people bid to have a character named after them.

7:00 pm - 8:00 pm

Director: Stephen Hopkins
Writers: Robert Cochran & Howard Gordon

Guest Cast: Xander Berkeley (George Mason), Daniel Bess (Rick), Navi Rawat (Melanie), Darin Heames (Krugman), Lou Diamond Phillips (Mark DeSalvo)

"I only hope your conscience comforts you when you finally realize this is all over." Sherry Palmer

Timeframe   Key Events

7:00 P.M. The helicopter departs. Jack and Mason find nothing. Mason is alerted that Alexis is awake and he leaves, while Jack stays. Tony takes a distraught Teri and wounded Parslow to CTU.

7:07 P.M. Kim is booked at the police station. Palmer is content with his decision and Sherry accuses him of giving up.

7:11 P.M. Jack finds a stairwell leading to a locked door. An alarm sounds, guards emerge from the door, taser Jack and drag him inside.

7:16 P.M. Jack wakes in a cell inside a top-secret underground detention facility, run by Department of Defense agent Mark DeSalvo. Jack details the Palmer assassination attempt and the power grid plan. Meanwhile, Andre Drazen readies his mercenaries.

7:19 P.M. A helicopter lands while Andre and his men wait for the power outage. The lights remain on and a hooded prisoner is ushered inside. Andre has to abandon the mission.

7:27 P.M. Kim is interrogated. She gives them the CTU number in desperation.

7:33 P.M. DeSalvo questions Jack's claims. Jack requests access to the prisoner. Denied, he calls Palmer to gain access.

7:36 P.M. Jack realizes the prisoner is Victor Drazen, alive and well.

7:43 P.M. Jack details to DeSalvo the entire Drazen revenge scheme. Andre prepares to blow up the electrical substation so he can get to his father.

7:46 P.M. Palmer tells Sherry their marriage is doomed and she tells him she will be his First Lady regardless.

7:54 P.M. DeSalvo gets a call from his superiors giving Jack permission to interrogate the prisoner. Jack begs Victor to call off the mission for the safety of his sons. DeSalvo agrees to move Victor.

7:59 P.M. As Victor is moved, the lights flicker and Drazen says, "They're here."

Jack is tasered.

Jack meets DeSalvo of DoD.

Jack recognizes Victor Drazen.

The episode where Tony saves Teri Bauer from the assassin ended up being pivotal for both Carlos Bernard and Leslie Hope. For Bernard, the episode was the first time Tony left the confines of CTU and proved himself as a hero. "When we were shooting the pilot, Joel and I talked about Tony, and Joel felt he really wanted the character to break out at some point." The moment finally came in the last third of the season, and it was an event Bernard felt was earned. "It was a turning point for Tony and it was really just written great. You couldn't ask for a better scene. It was also the moment when the audience finally trusted him, even though, I think, towards the end of the season people were still thinking he might turn," he smiles.

On the flip side, Tony saving Teri also triggered the return of her memory, sending the character off into an emotional tailspin. It proved to be one of the most difficult scenes for Leslie

Hope. "I was really challenged when Tony came to get me. I think all over again that Kim is dead and I had to completely lose my s*** again," she sighs. "I remember it was 2 am, it was cold and it just felt like I had done this over and over again. I remember thinking the challenge was that I couldn't fake my way through it. Sometimes as an actor on other shows, you can fake it, right? You can sort of do smoke and mirrors and say 'Look over here', but we couldn't do that on 24 due to the nature of the show. And I remember thinking, 'I don't know if I can pull this off or not.' Again, it wasn't that I didn't think it was right for the character, but I wasn't sure I could physically do it."

Research Files

Underground Detention Facilities: Department of Defense agent Mark DeSalvo talks to Jack after he awakens inside a holding cell in the class-three underground detention center. Typically, underground prison facilities are mostly attributed to foreign countries holding prisoners of war. Vietnam was one of the nations using this type of detention and many US soldiers came back from the Vietnam War with tales of their incarceration in these uniquely hostile environments. There are no official sub-surface prisons in the United States, but there is an underground city known as The Facility, built in the 1950s by the Federal Emergency Management Agency (FEMA) to house the surviving members of government in the aftermath of a nuclear attack. Situated below the solid granite of Mount Weather in Bluemont, Virginia, it reportedly cost over $1 billion.

Additional Intel

Kiefer Sutherland trying to drag Dennis Hopper off to jail isn't a new on-screen dynamic for the actors, as the pair played out a similar situation in the 1990 film, *Flashback*. In it, Sutherland was an uptight FBI agent assigned to bring Hopper's former hippie-radical to prison.

8:00 pm - 9:00 pm

Director: Stephen Hopkins
Writers: Joel Surnow & Michael Loceff

Guest Cast: Zeljko Ivanek (Andre Drazen), Jude Ciccolella (Mike Novick), Lou Diamond Phillips (Mark DeSalvo), Dennis Hopper (Victor Drazen)

> "You take all the bad luck you've had in your entire life, it wouldn't fit into half of what's happened to me in the past twenty-four hours…"
> Kim Bauer

Timeframe   Key Events

8:00 P.M. Kim and Melanie have a confrontation.

8:03 P.M. Palmer wins the Super Tuesday Primary election.

8:06 P.M. Jack calls Nina and Mason answers. Jack explains the Drazen issue and begs for backup, which Mason grants. Tony and Teri arrive at CTU.

8:08 P.M. Jack and DeSalvo lead Drazen away and an explosion rocks the compound.

8:17 P.M. Campaign manager Patty Brooks and Palmer finish writing his victory speech.

8:19 P.M. Andre Drazen's team enters the detention facility hallway to find Jack with his gun trained on Victor. Andre takes DeSalvo at gunpoint. Jack relents, but Andre kills DeSalvo. Andre and Victor take Jack hostage.

8:29 P.M. Mason refuses to negotiate with Victor, who puts Jack on the phone to prove he is alive. Jack gives Mason a quick situation assessment and Victor yanks the phone away.

8:34 P.M. Jack realizes Victor sent a decoy into the building in Kosovo. Victor lets his guard down for a moment and Jack knocks him down. Andre beats Jack senseless.

8:40 P.M. Patty watches Palmer prepare and offers to massage his back.

8:43 P.M. Mason finally gets hold of CTU Director Ryan Chappelle, who demands that Mason immediately end the situation at the facility.

8:46 P.M. Tony lets Teri know Kim is safe, but Nina has to tell her Jack is being held hostage.

8:53 P.M. Nina hears Mason order the CTU units to apprehend Victor Drazen even at the expense of Jack.

8:55 P.M. The troops can't find Jack. The Drazens emerge outside, ready to kill Jack, but he offers to help them get Alexis. Victor agrees and they load him into a van.

8:59 P.M. Kim is on her way to her mother in a squad car, which is smashed into by a van. Three Serbian men grab Kim.

An explosion rocks the compound.

Jack takes Victor hostage.

Kim is kidnapped by masked men.

Casting directors Debi Manwiller and Peggy Kennedy are responsible for selecting all the actors cast on *24*. During season one, the character of Victor Drazen became one of the first high profile guest roles written for the show. Fortunately, legendary Hollywood film and TV actor Dennis Hopper ably filled the shoes of the ruthless Serbian patriarch. Remembering the casting process, Kennedy says, "We had cast the Drazen family prior to having Dennis Hopper. The network wanted us to think in terms of a more recognizable name for what we called the 'end game' character, which was Victor. After checking availabilities, Dennis's name came up and was one that jumped out at us." With the series still building an audience, Manwiller remembers they had to work to get Hopper to understand the concept of *24* and woo him to the role. "I think he was intrigued. At that time, we had to pitch the whole

concept of the show. He was a character that we were looking for a couple of months ahead of actually using him, so nothing had been finalized. We had to explain to him what the show was, and that we didn't know exactly what he would be doing. We knew he would do a few episodes; the producers had that much in their heads. There was a meeting that took place where the producers pitched the character to him, what it was going to be, and then they said they would write it. We didn't have a script to send him — that's the crazy part! He had to go on faith, and I believe we had a closed deal before we even had a completed script."

Research Files

Super Tuesday: The Palmers await the results of the primaries of Super Tuesday to see if the Senator will secure enough delegate votes to win the party's official nomination as their candidate for President. In the race for the White House, the primary election is a method by which a political party chooses its nominee for President. The winners of primary elections run against nominees of other parties in the general election. The phrase 'Super Tuesday' first came into use for the slate of primary elections that took place on 8 March 1988, when nine Southern states were hosting primary votes.

Additional Intel

The *24* producers cast another of Kiefer's former big screen collaborators, Lou Diamond Phillips, in the role of Mark DeSalvo. The actors appeared together in the films *Young Guns*, *Renegades* and *Young Guns II*.

9:00 pm - 10:00 pm

Director: Paul Shapiro
Writers: Joel Surnow & Michael Loceff

Guest Cast: Zeljko Ivanek (Andre Drazen), Misha Collins (Alexis Drazen), Tanya Wright (Patty Brooks), Dennis Hopper (Victor Drazen)

"Jack's on his own. I'm sorry." Nina Myers

Timeframe

9:00 P.M. Palmer gives a rousing speech. Victor says he will trade Jack for Alexis. Mason says he is not authorized to do that.

9:08 P.M. Mason tells Nina that Chappelle will not allow the trade. Nina tells Teri.

9:15 P.M. The Drazens take Jack to the basement of a Slavic restaurant to hide.

9:19 P.M. Teri goes to Nina who has a plan. Nina places an urgent call to Palmer about the situation. Tony finds out Kim has been taken again and tells Nina.

9:26 P.M. Palmer calls Mason and demands that the trade be allowed. Palmer promises Mason a huge promotion when he is elected. Jack takes a waitress hostage with a knife to gain an advantage, but Victor shoots her.

9:29 P.M. Andre calls Mason and the trade is agreed upon. Mason goes to collect Alexis from the hospital.

9:31 P.M. The tension between Palmer and Sherry increases. Patty and Palmer flirt and they arrange to meet upstairs.

9:34 P.M. Kim is dragged into the basement and Jack is taken away for the exchange.

9:39 P.M. Teri is relieved at the news, but doesn't know about Kim.

9:42 P.M. Jack begs for Kim's life.

9:45 P.M. Jack is tethered to a post in an oil field with snipers positioned on him. A cell phone is placed in his pocket.

9:51 P.M. At the campaign party, Sherry conspires with Patty about Palmer. Patty is uncomfortable lying, but Sherry says it's for the greater good.

9:54 P.M. Mason hands over Alexis to the Drazens' guard, Harris, and demands Jack be released too. Once Harris is sure they aren't being followed, he will give Jack's location. Mason agrees and calls Nina to track Harris' SUV.

9:58 P.M. The trace attached to Alexis is found and destroyed.

9:59 P.M. Andre gives the signal to release Jack. His cell rings and he is directed to a new location if he wants Kim.

Key Events

Jack takes a waitress hostage.

Patty and Sherry conspire about Palmer.

Mason hands over Alexis.

While the producers had figured out Nina was the mole earlier in the season, they didn't tell anyone until the last four episodes. "I had no clue about Nina being the mole," Sarah Clarke laughs. "I was naïve. I was thinking, 'Yeah, I love Jack. I'm the one who helps him.' I remember wondering, 'How are they going to surprise everyone?' I thought the mole might have been Tony, but that seemed too obvious. Literally, I think I got the news four episodes from the end of the season. When they told me I was blindsided, for sure. I remember thinking, 'How is that going to play?' and I went back and looked at the episodes and sure enough it tracked. Then I was really excited. Talking to Joel and fleshing it out, it made perfect sense that I was a great double agent. I loved the duplicity of having a mission, but then falling for people along the way. Truly, I think Nina loved Jack. I like to think Nina was a pretty good person and she

just made some really bad mistakes and then it just spiraled.

"I really like Leslie Hope, so I was sad I was making her character end," Clarke continues. "Although, at that point, we all had no idea what incarnation the show would come back in. The producers had talked about the show going backwards, so we all could come back no matter what. They also talked at one point about making the show an ensemble piece, where it was another twenty-four hours, but we all played different people. There were different thoughts being thrown around about what they were going to do, so no one really took it like it was over for Teri. And it was also up in the air if they were going to kill her or not."

Research Files

Börek: Victor Drazen taunts Jack Bauer by tasting a piece of Börek. A traditional dish originating from Turkey and especially popular with people in the Balkan regions, Börek is made of filo pastry and is generally filled with feta cheese, ground beef, and/or vegetables (most commonly spinach). Börek is a regular staple offered at local bakeries, and is the equivalent of fast food in those countries. It is also often consumed with yogurt.

Additional Intel

During the first season of the show, both Mac and PC format computers were featured on the show. What some people didn't realize was that the bad guys for the season were always seen using PC computers and the good guys were all using Mac computers.

10:00 pm - 11:00 pm

Director: Paul Shapiro
Writers: Robert Cochran & Howard Gordon

Guest Cast: Zeljko Ivanek (Andre Drazen), Xander Berkeley (George Mason), Misha Collins (Alexis Drazen), Dennis Hopper (Victor Drazen)

> "I promise you, everything is gonna be okay. It's just been a… a really, really long day."
> Jack Bauer

Timeframe	Key Events

10:00 P.M. Andre wants the Senator to unfreeze $200 million of the Drazens' assets and then Jack will kill Palmer.

10:06 P.M. Mason has Nina try to find the SUV. Jack calls and says he can't come in. The CTU team surmises that the Drazens are using Jack to kill Palmer. The Secret Service is alerted. Meanwhile, Alexis arrives, but dies from his injuries. Andre is furious, and wants Jack to suffer.

10:14 P.M. Patty tells Sherry about the meeting with Palmer. Tony finds the detention facility schematic was tampered with, alerting them to another dirty agent.

10:19 P.M. Jack phones Palmer and asks to see him, to relay a message from Victor. Jack promises that he will not harm him.

10:25 P.M. Palmer meets Patty in the hotel suite, where he fires her for conspiring with his wife against him. Nina and Tony wonder if Mason is the mole. Nina orders Tony to shut down Mason's security access.

10:29 P.M. Jack asks Palmer to cooperate to save Kim. The cell phone from Drazen rings and Palmer answers it. Jack smells a trap, throws the phone out the window and it explodes. Palmer and Jack are unhurt, but the Drazens think it worked.

10:37 P.M. Sherry finds Palmer alive but Jack asks them to pretend the Senator was killed, in order to save Kim.

10:40 P.M. CTU sees a report Palmer is dead. The Drazens call the suite to confirm, but Jack answers. He asks to be traded for Kim. They tell him to meet them at the Port of Los Angeles.

10:53 P.M. Mason tells Nina and Tony that Palmer survived.

10:54 P.M. Kim throws hot coffee on the guard watching her and escapes. She jumps in the water, where she hides under the dock.

10:59 P.M. Andre's cell phone rings. A woman named Yelena says in Serbian that Palmer is still alive. Yelena is revealed to be Nina Myers.

Alexis Drazen dies.

Jack protects Palmer from a bomb.

Nina is revealed as the mole.

Co-creator Joel Surnow admits crafting the first season of *24* was a very organic process. With such a unique format, the network also had a lot of input on what they wanted to see from the creative team. "One of the first concerns of the network was that the show have a standalone quality," Surnow remembers. "They said every episode should have a beginning, middle and an end and that's it — but that's just not organic. We made sure there were little mini-stories within the hour that played out, but we always felt that cliffhangers were the key to the show. It would have been a lot harder without them because you are doing an ongoing story, and it's your natural inclination to keep the story going. I think we had some episodes that ended on a downbeat note, where it was paying off something in that episode that didn't take you to the next place; but after a while we realized it was better not to run away from the organic nature

of the show, which is to keep the story moving forward."

Surnow also reveals that those cliffhangers are arrived at in a multitude of different ways, rather than the linear plot development audiences might expect. "We come up with different pieces of the story at different times. We are all about coming up with those standalone, set-piece scenes that will make the audience go 'Holy s***!' The big thing with *24* is the '*24* moments'. Everyone can tell you their favorite scenes, like Alan York killing Janet, so we try to write scripts to accomplish that. Early on, we were told, 'No cliffhangers'. By the end of the first year, heading into the second year, the network mandate was, 'Make sure you have those cliffhangers!' They are what makes *24* different," he laughs.

Research Files

Coast Guard: Jack contacts the Coast Guard to claim the body of his daughter, Kim Bauer, who was supposedly found floating in the waters of the Port of Los Angeles. The United States Coast Guard is a military service operating under the United States Department of Homeland Security (as of 2003) in peacetime and reporting to the Secretary of the Navy during wartime. It is the smallest armed service of the US military and deals with law enforcement on the seas, search and rescue, marine environmental pollution response and the maintenance of local rivers and navigations. The Coast Guard originally began as the Revenue Cutter Service, founded on 4 August 1790 as part of the Department of the Treasury.

Additional Intel

Over the course of twenty-four episodes, fifty-nine deaths occurred on screen, including major characters, recurring characters and minor henchmen. The first death was Victor Rovner in Kuala Lumpur and the last was Teri Bauer.

11:00 pm - 12:00 am

Director: Stephen Hopkins
Story: Robert Cochran & Joel Surnow
Teleplay: Joel Surnow & Michael Loceff

Guest Cast: Zeljko Ivanek (Andre Drazen), Jude Ciccolella (Mike Novick), Terrell Tilford (Paul Wilson), Dennis Hopper (Victor Drazen)

"How many people died because of you, Jack?"
Nina Myers

Timeframe	Key Events

11:00 P.M. Mason gets a call from Kim. Jack arrives at the port. Andre knows Palmer is still alive. Jack calls Nina to confirm a mole in CTU. Nina doesn't let Jack know that Kim is safe.

11:11 P.M. The news confirms Palmer is alive: Sherry leaked the truth.

11:17 P.M. Victor orders Nina to tell Jack that Kim's body was found in the water and Jack clicks into revenge mode.

11:20 P.M. Jack plows a van through the warehouse wall. He shoots Andre dead, but Victor wounds Jack. Jack advances and Victor, out of ammo, surrenders — hands raised. Jack pauses and unloads a clip into Victor.

11:28 P.M. Palmer apologizes to the press for the confusion about his 'death'.

11:31 P.M. Nina hears Jack took out the Drazens. She slips out to the transformer room, makes a call in German and says she's been compromised. Teri walks in and gets suspicious. Nina pulls a gun on Teri.

11:35 P.M. Jack finds out Kim isn't dead and Mason confirms her safety. Jack figures out that Nina is the mole, but Mason says he needs proof to arrest her.

11:42 P.M. Palmer tells Sherry he never wants to see her again, and leaves the marriage.

11:46 P.M. Jack gets video footage that shows Nina murdered Jamey and sends it to Mason.

11:53 P.M. Nina makes her getaway, leaving Teri behind. Nina kills two guards and is about to escape when Jack arrives. They race at one another full throttle and Nina swerves and crashes. Jack drags her out of the car with a gun at her head. Mason, Tony and others yell that they need her alive. He lowers his gun and Nina is arrested.

11:58 P.M. Jack is reunited with Kim and he goes to find Teri.

11:59 P.M. Jack finds Teri dead with multiple bullets in her abdomen. Jack sinks to the floor with her lifeless body and breaks down in utter grief.

Jack breaks down after killing the Drazens.

Nina looks down the barrel of Jack's gun.

Jack cradles his wife's dead body.

The murder of Teri Bauer in the season finale was truly a watershed moment for the series in terms of defining the risks the producers would take to tell the best story. Unfortunately, it meant the loss of Leslie Hope. "I am always the person who is the last to believe that something is going to work," Hope reveals. "I was the last one to believe that the pilot would get picked up. When it got picked up for thirteen, I thought it would never get picked up for twenty-four; so when it got picked up for twenty-four, I was like, 'Wow, really?' It was around the same time that I got pregnant on the show and I was like, 'Well, if I'm pregnant, then for sure I'm around for season two because I'm the pregnant wife of the hero!'" she laughs.

The producers considerately gave Hope early warning of her demise. "I knew about it a month or so before we shot it." Yet, still, the ending was shot two different ways, one with Teri alive

(which can be seen on the Season One DVD) and then the way it actually aired. "When you see them side-by-side, it's so clear and evident I should be dead," Hope laughs. "The other one just looks hokey especially when you know the alternative is so much better."

Remembering the actual scene where Jack cradles Teri's body in his arms, Hope reveals, "For me it was emotional, not because it was the end of my time in the show but because Kiefer was so terrific in the scene. When we were shooting it, you can't tell because of the way it's shot, but there are tears coming down my face because he was so good. It's really great television, and surprising in the best way. It makes sense and alerts you that the show is not going to follow the rules of a standard series. I think ultimately it was a great, great move on their part."

Research Files

Mole: Jack Bauer learns that Nina Myers was the mole working at CTU for the Drazens. The term mole is commonly used to describe a spy working in one organization, seeking and gaining access to confidential information that will be passed to another organization for which the person actually works. Francis Bacon first coined and used the term 'mole' in 1626 for his work *History of the Reign of King Henry VII*. Moles are actually quite rare in high-level espionage due to the long amount of time and preparation needed to gain access to the inner circles of security and information.

Additional Intel

Leslie Hope admits she didn't know Teri's actual fate until the night the season finale aired. "They didn't let me know officially until right before it aired because I think *they* actually didn't know. It's the only episode that I haven't watched. The night it aired, I had dinner with Kiefer."

DAY TWO

Regular Cast:
Kiefer Sutherland (Jack Bauer)
Sarah Wynter (Kate Warner)
Elisha Cuthbert (Kimberly Bauer)
Xander Berkeley (George Mason)
Carlos Bernard (Tony Almeida)
Dennis Haysbert (President David Palmer)
Penny Johnson Jerald (Sherry Palmer)

8:00 am - 9:00 am

Director: Jon Cassar
Writers: Joel Surnow & Michael Loceff

Guest Cast: Vicellous Reon Shannon (Keith Palmer), Skye McCole Bartusiak (Megan Matheson), Michelle Forbes (Lynne Kresge), Sara Gilbert (Paula Schaeffer)

"I'd start rolling up your sleeves. I'm gonna need a hacksaw." Jack Bauer

Timeframe   Key Events

8:00 A.M. In Korea, a tortured man says, "today". NSA staffer Eric Rayburn is called.

8:02 A.M. On vacation in Oregon, President Palmer is whisked away by his advisors. In LA, Kim Bauer nannies for nine-year-old Megan Matheson.

8:06 A.M. At CTU, George Mason is asked by Rayburn to bring Jack Bauer back in.

8:08 A.M. Rayburn meets Palmer and his aide, Lynne Kresge, at the Northwest Regional Operations Complex. He reveals that a nuclear bomb is set to detonate in LA today. Potential suicide bomber Mamud Rashed Faheen of Second Wave is suspected.

8:12 A.M. Palmer calls the Prime Minister of a Middle Eastern state, unofficially linked with Second Wave, to warn of the terrorists' intent, and threatens to retaliate if the bomb is detonated.

8:16 A.M. Jack talks to Kim, who has been estranged since Teri's death. A Middle Eastern man, Reza Naiyeer, greets the family of his fiancée, Marie Warner.

8:24 A.M. Jack ignores his CTU messages. Palmer calls. Jack answers and is persuaded to return to CTU.

8:28 A.M. CTU staffer Michelle Dessler tells Tony the CIA issued an Information Flow Advisory.

8:31 A.M. Mason briefs CTU on the threat.

8:36 A.M. Arabic men in LA prepare the bomb. Jack arrives at CTU and is briefed. He immediately calls Kim and demands Mason has two agents take her out of town. Mason says Jack's former arrest, Joseph Wald, is connected to Second Wave. Jack demands key witness Marshall Goren be brought in.

8:46 A.M. A private investigator warns the Warners about Reza's link to terrorists. Rayburn sets up a meeting with the Joint Chiefs of Staff. Palmer cancels it and reprimands him.

8:49 A.M. Goren arrives. Jack pulls out a gun, shoots Goren in the chest and asks for a hacksaw. Mason freaks out.

8:59 A.M. Megan's father, Gary, a domestic abuser, beats his wife, Carla; and then attacks his daughter while Kim tries to protect her. Jack shaves and goes back to work.

The terrorists prepare the bomb.

Jack shoots Goren at CTU.

Jack is back to fight again.

For season two of *24*, the producers decided to blend extremist terrorism and a nuclear bomb threat for the crisis of the day. While many critics and fans assumed that *24* was modeling its second season on events going on in the real world, especially paralleling the start of the war in Iraq, Joel Surnow refutes that assertion entirely. "We got a little weirdly synchronized during season two when we were ramping up for war on the show, and we were ramping up for war in the United States. That was just an accidental thing. It was just a matter of timing." Executive producer Evan Katz continues, "The second season had a lot to do with fomenting a war under false pretences in the Middle East. We had no idea we were going to war with Iraq at that time, so it was completely predictive on our part that something like that could happen. It felt very eerie at the time. It was in the planning stages long before, and had been in the can for

some time, so to speak. We knew people would think we were commenting on the war, but we weren't. In fact, we try not to get too close to current events because we feel it is distracting. We don't want to be allied with contemporary politics or political events. We don't want to be seen as commenting on it. It's about heroism and not about who is in the White House or what war America happens to be involved in."

Surnow says showing Middle Eastern terrorists on domestic soil was a challenge, too. "We had one of our characters go into a mosque to find a terrorist. I think because it was so close to 9/11, some of the Muslim groups didn't feel they could voice a protest, but even in that season, we showed both sides. We showed really positive Muslim families and that a Muslim accused of being a terrorist in fact wasn't. It's unrealistic to do too much about terrorism without dealing with the Muslim issue. The issues that we deal with are the issues that are here, right now, present day. We haven't really veered from that and they continue to be timely."

Research Files

Nuclear Bomb: President Palmer is notified of a threat of a rogue nuclear bomb exploding in Los Angeles. The first nuclear weapons were created in the United States during World War Two as part of a top secret initiative dubbed the Manhattan Project. The first bombs released during warfare were against the Japanese cities of Hiroshima and Nagasaki in August 1945, which killed at least 120,000 people instantly, with many more dying from radiation after-effects. A nuclear bomb derives its incredible destructive force from the nuclear reactions of fission and fusion. There are an estimated 29,000 nuclear weapons in the world held by more than seven countries.

Additional Intel

In the scene where Jack shoots Goren, director of photography Rodney Charters admits he came up with Jack's bone-chilling, "I'm gonna need a hacksaw" while they were shooting. Despite the network's concern, the now classic line remained in the final edit.

9:00 am - 10:00 am

Director: Jon Cassar
Writers: Joel Surnow & Michael Loceff

Guest Cast: Reiko Aylesworth (Michelle Dessler), Billy Burke (Gary Matheson), Tamlyn Tomita (Jenny Dodge), Tracy Middendorf (Carla Matheson)

"Jack's Back." Eddie Grant

Timeframe

Key Events

9:00 A.M. Palmer does not want any leaks that will lead to mass hysteria. The bomb is loaded into a van. Kim Bauer goes on the run with Megan.

9:05 A.M. Jack is transported by helicopter and briefed about Wald's crew. Jack recognizes Eddie Grant. Jack demands no agency interference. Jack calls Kim to tell her to leave LA.

9:09 A.M. Jack meets with Eddie, who accuses him of putting Wald in jail. Jack gets back in favor by showing Eddie Goren's head in a bag. Eddie smiles.

9:16 A.M. Palmer dodges the press about his canceled vacation.

9:20 A.M. Eddie takes Jack to Dave, who is suspicious. CTU is slow uploading Jack's fake profile into the system, which causes a tense moment before it finally appears.

9:28 A.M. Rayburn hounds Palmer about military action. Lynne says reporter Ron Wieland is doing a story on the Alert Condition change. Palmer asks to talk to him and Richard Armus.

9:31 A.M. Jack asks to see Joe Wald, but Eddie says he is busy. Jack floods his car so he can stick around longer.

9:33 A.M. Mason sees the probability of attack is eighty-nine to ninety-three percent so he packs up and leaves to follow up a lead in Bakersfield.

9:40 A.M. Kim and Megan hide. Kate Warner searches for Reza's passport.

9:45 A.M. Dave gives Jack a hard time. The two fight. Jack breaks Dave's ankle.

9:50 A.M. Kim calls 911 at a payphone. Gary shows up and gets forceful with Kim. She cracks him with a tire iron and runs.

9:54 A.M. Palmer asks Wieland to sit on the Alert story. Palmer has Armus drag Wieland away.

9:57 A.M. Eddie recruits Jack to replace Dave. Kim loses Megan.

9:59 A.M. Jack asks about the job and Eddie says they are bringing down CTU.

Kim is told to run with Megan.

Jack drops off Goran's head.

Palmer talks to Ron about his story.

Casting director Debi Manwiller says casting the part of Kim Bauer's young charge, Megan Matheson, was relatively easy, despite the inherent challenges of finding a young actor who could rise to the dramatic demands of the series. "We had seen Skye McCole Bartusiak in *The Cider House Rules* just as our season was coming up. She is a good actress, just the real deal. There are always a few out there, like Skye and Dakota Fanning, at any given time. We lucked out with her and didn't end up seeing tons of kids. We brought her in really early on and it was like, 'Okay, done!'"

Kim Bauer was caught up in the domestic abuse storyline for the first third of the season. While it gave her a purpose, it also kept Kim away from her father's world and the main jeopardy of the story. "Somehow she turned into this very reactive character, as opposed to being very proactive, in the things she

did for the season," Elisha Cuthbert says about the character's struggles that year. "Here I was, the daughter in the situation, and the writers were trying to figure out how to incorporate her into saving the world. It was a difficult thing to do. At first I found myself running around and taking care of a small child. The reason why we did that was to show that Kim was older and more mature. But, looking back, I think the second season was difficult for everyone. I don't think anyone was ready to come back, because everyone thought the first season would be so unique and so different for television, coming back wouldn't even be an option. I was making a movie during that season too; I was going back and forth from *The Girl Next Door* to night shoots at *24*. But I put a lot of time and work into that year, so I am proud of it."

Research Files

Terror Alert: As President Palmer and his aides evaluate the terrorists' aims, they discuss whether the terror alert color should be adjusted. The Homeland Security Advisory System was created six months after the 11 September 2001 terrorist attacks. The color-coded scale reflects alert status around the country and changes affect federal agencies, state and local government actions, and specifically security at airports and other public facilities, like tourist attractions or important buildings. The color scale is as follows: red (severe), orange (high), yellow (elevated), blue (guarded), and green (low). The American military already has a threat level advisory system called LERTCON, which is broken down into five Defense Conditions (DEFCONs) and two Emergency Conditions (EMERGCONs).

Additional Intel

Day two of *24* takes place eighteen months after the March California Presidential Primary, which, chronologically, places this day in September.

10:00 am - 11:00 am

Director: James Whitmore Jr.
Writer: Howard Gordon

Guest Cast: Reiko Aylesworth (Michelle Dessler), John Terry (Bob Warner), Timothy Carhart (Eric Rayburn), Sara Gilbert (Paula Schaeffer)

"I'm never going to let him hurt you again."
Kim Bauer

Timeframe

10:00 A.M. Gary tells the police Kim kidnapped Megan. Tony tells Mason to follow up in Panorama City. Lynne tells Palmer NSA believes they are looking for a nuke. Jack questions Eddie, but then Kim calls begging for his help. He tells her to go to Aunt Carol's. Kim calls CTU and Tony explains Jack is undercover.

10:08 A.M. Eddie's crew corrupts the CTU phones. Jack calls Palmer.

10:11 A.M. Lynne takes Jack's call and he says: evacuate CTU. Rayburn stops Lynne from alerting CTU for fear of blowing Jack's cover. Eddie's team ambushes the telephone workers.

10:16 A.M. Rayburn tells Tony to transfer all threat data to the NSA server. Michelle points out that CTU was the only agency given that request.

10:22 A.M. Mason arrives in Panorama City, where the bomb was built. A shootout occurs in the warehouse and powder is dispersed — a radiation warning sign. It's a hot zone. Kim gets Megan and they ride a bus to CTU. Eddie and Jack's crew sneak into CTU as telephone repairmen.

10:30 A.M. Kate Warner's private investigator confirms Reza did have contact with the terrorists. He must alert Homeland Security and warns her to keep quiet.

10:34 A.M. Eddie enters CTU. Jack stays behind and writes a note warning about bombs in the building.

10:41 A.M. Mason updates Tony and sends him the fingerprints of the shooters.

10:44 A.M. Jack leaves the note on the telephone worker and explains it's for Tony. Jack injures himself as a ploy. Eddie and the team leave. Kim and Megan arrive asking for Tony.

10:54 A.M. Rayburn threatens Lynne not to cross him. Palmer tells Lynne to alert CTU. Tony gets Jack's note and orders immediate evacuation. The building explodes.

10:59 A.M. Mason is informed he inhaled plutonium and has one day left to live.

Key Events

Mason is exposed to the radiation hot zone.

Kim and Megan arrive at CTU.

CTU is bombed.

Stan and Scott Blackwell are twin brothers who have worked together or individually supervising the wide variety of special effects needed on *24* since the pilot. Their team is responsible for everything from the squib detonations when a character is shot, all the way up to the impressive explosions, crashes and shootouts featured in each season. "The best thing about this show is that the crew is great," Stan offers. "It's a tight group of people and we've learned to trust each other. The camera guys even ask us where they can be and where they are safe."

For the massively dramatic bombing of CTU in the early part of the second season, Scott Blackwell was away working on the movie *The Last Samurai*, so Stan was the mastermind of that particular sequence, or "gag" as professional special effects people call them. "It was originally scripted as a huge fireball that washes through CTU," Stan remembers. Shot at their former

Woodland Hills soundstages, the scope of the gag meant working around the many limitations of the environment. "In buildings like that, there are sprinkler systems. If you create a fireball, the fire has to go somewhere, so we would have had to put a hole in the roof to let the fire escape without setting off the sprinkler systems. So we talked about it a lot and decided to do the sequence a different way. In the end, with all the different bits of glass shattering and the fake walls blowing up, there were actually ninety-three separate explosions in that sequence. It was a challenge, but I think it came off pretty good."

Research Files

NSA: The National Security Agency, or NSA (as represented in the show by staffers Rayburn and Stanton) is the largest United States government intelligence agency, responsible for collecting and analyzing foreign communications from around the world to assess global security and risk. The NSA works closely with the Department of Defense and is typically directed by a military officer. Headquarters are based in Fort Mead, Maryland. The NSA was created in June 1952 by the Executive Order of the then-President of the United States, Harry S. Truman.

Additional Intel

Reiko Aylesworth originally auditioned for Sarah Clarke's role as Nina Myers. She came back in season two to read for Sarah Wynter's role of Kate Warner, but was instead cast as CTU's Michelle Dessler, becoming a regular cast member in season three.

11:00 am - 12:00 pm

Director: James Whitmore Jr.
Writer: Remi Aubuchon

Guest Cast: Reiko Aylesworth (Michelle Dessler), Billy Burke (Gary Matheson), Phillip Rhys (Reza Naiyeer), Scott Allan Campbell (Hazmat Dr. Porter)

"I'm doing my job. You people better start doing yours!" Jack Bauer

Timeframe   Key Events

11:00 A.M. Eddie's team listens to the scanner for casualties. Jack is livid. Tony is alive. Kim and Megan are safe, but then Megan starts to have seizures. Paramedics take Megan.

11:03 A.M. Palmer is upset about the CTU bombing. Lynne blames Rayburn for the casualties, but he turns it around and blackmails her.

11:05 A.M. In Panorama city Mason learns from an EMT what his deterioration will be like. Tony calls Mason about the bombing. CTU staffer Paula is injured and can't decrypt the nuclear intelligence. Mason orders them to get that data, and says he may not be back. Tony is furious.

11:08 A.M. Joe Wald calls Eddie and gives him an address. Jack pulls a gun, demands the address and arrests Eddie. The crew fires on Jack but he kills them all and takes the car.

11:16 A.M. Jack calls CTU. Michelle talks to Jack and he asks about Kim. She tells Tony and they search for her. At the hospital, Kim learns Megan has a skull fracture from her domestic abuse.

11:21 A.M. Palmer and his advisors watch reports on the CTU bomb. Rayburn suggests a city evacuation, but the President orders no evacuation. Kate Warner tells her father the information about Reza. He asks her to accept Reza, but she is worried.

11:29 A.M. Jack calls OC and blames Lynne for the deaths.

11:30 A.M. Jack goes to the address and finds Wald. A pit bull attacks Jack. Wald runs and locks himself in a secured room.

11:34 A.M. Kim calls Carla about Megan. They verbally fight and then Carla heads to the hospital, but Gary stops her. Jack pleads with Wald.

11:42 A.M. Reza shows Kate the home he has bought Marie.

11:45 A.M. Mason arrives and fights with Tony about how to handle the injured Paula.

11:55 A.M. Palmer fires Rayburn and sends him to Armus.

11:57 A.M. Jack gets Wald to tell him who ordered the CTU hit. He gives Jack a photo of Nina Myers.

Jack stands down Eddie's car.

Palmer fires Rayburn.

Nina Myers is revealed as Wald's contact.

Actor Carlos Bernard's character Tony Almeida was right in the middle of the CTU destruction, with the walls of the compound literally raining down on him on the day of the shoot. "It was a very memorable day because there wasn't a lot of acting going on," he laughs. "They set off some major explosions in there and really all you had to do was let yourself react to it. I remember being on one side of the set during the explosion and being hit and pelted with stuff from the other side — and it's a huge set."

A life-long Cubs fan, Bernard thought a Cubs mug would be a good addition to Tony's desk at CTU. "I brought it in during the very first episode to put on my desk because I thought this is a guy who is very strategically minded, and I thought he would be a big baseball fan. I put it in there for the Chicago people watching, too," he smiles. "When we blew up CTU, they were going to

Research Files

Radiation Exposure: CTU Director George Mason is exposed to active plutonium from the nuclear bomb and succumbs to radiation poisoning, or 'radiation sickness', an intense form of damage to living tissue due to excessive exposure to ionizing radiation. Intense exposure particularly affects and interferes with cell division. Dosimeters are an effective monitor of a person's total exposure to radiation, and are used at all facilities where nuclear power is used or handled. Eighty percent of any plutonium that enters the bloodstream goes either to the liver or into the bones.

Additional Intel

A reputed practical joker on the set, Carlos Bernard admits he likes to mess with Kiefer Sutherland's concentration. One of his favorite things to do, right before the director calls action, is to say a name or word that Kiefer has to say in the scene, but say it incorrectly, so Sutherland can't get it right during the take.

have me find the Cubs mug broken." Bernard agreed to this and on the day of the bombing, they set up a shot to destroy the mug. "Jon Cassar said, 'Okay, let's break it!' So I took the mug and winged it straight up in the air, way up, and was going to let it drop on the cement and break. But it got caught in the wires and didn't come down! So we decided the Cubs mug should live. The gods spared it so we kept it and it has appeared in every season since."

12:00 pm - 1:00 pm

Director: Jon Cassar
Writer: Gil Grant

Guest Cast: Reiko Aylesworth (Michelle Dessler), Michelle Forbes (Lynne Kresge), Sara Gilbert (Paula Schaeffer), Sarah Clarke (Nina Myers)

"Ralph Burton is a PI. He could probably connect me to the Manson family if he looked hard enough." Bob Warner

Timeframe

12:00 P.M. Jack calls Mason about Nina and wants her at CTU. Mason says he will handle her.

12:04 P.M. The bomb moves closer to the target. Kim sees Gary at the hospital and he tells her to leave or they will charge her with abuse.

12:07 P.M. Roger Stanton, the head of NSA, apologizes to Palmer for Rayburn.

12:09 P.M. Jack returns to CTU. Mason is angry and tells him to leave after his debrief.

12:17 P.M. Paula provides her decryption key to complete the file transmission to NSA and then dies. Tony arrives at the Warner house to question Reza.

12:21 P.M. The Ambassador tells Palmer they want to help prevent the bomb. Stanton and Lynne don't trust the Ambassador, and strongly believe that they do support Second Wave. Palmer is torn.

12:25 P.M. Kim calls Jack. He warns her about the bomb threat and tells her to run, he will meet her later. Jack then watches Nina return in shackles to CTU.

12:32 P.M. Mason interrogates Nina and she requests a full Presidential Pardon in return for her assistance. Mason dismisses Jack. Reza denies knowing terrorist Syed Ali.

12:36 P.M. Palmer provides their intel to the Ambassador and Stanton is uneasy. Kim calls her boyfriend Miguel to pick her up.

12:39 P.M. Palmer calls Jack to tell him he had to grant the pardon to help avert the crisis.

12:44 P.M. Jack asks to interrogate Nina. Mason refuses, then tries to take his medication, but Jack swipes it.

12:47 P.M. Jack knows something is wrong with Mason and questions if he is fit to lead CTU.

12:54 P.M. Kim tells Miguel about the bomb and he promises to help her and Megan. Jack forces Mason to allow him to talk to Nina or he will tell Division Mason is sick. The Ambassador's helicopter crashes.

12:59 P.M. Jack prepares to face Nina.

Key Events

Paula gives the code before she dies.

Kim calls Jack.

The Ambassador's helicopter goes down.

When Nina Myers was carted off to prison for treason and the murder of Teri Bauer at the end of season one, audiences knew it would just be a matter of time before she returned to confront Jack Bauer once again. For actress Sarah Clarke, stepping back into character for this arc was exactly what she was hoping for. "After the first season, you realize, on a show like this, that storylines can get extended to such a point that they become ridiculous. I was just getting to the stage of feeling the repetition of, 'Where's Jack now and how can I help him?' and then I was the mole, and that gave me a whole new thing. When they told me I was coming back, I knew that my story was going to be amazing because, however I was coming back, it wasn't going to be extended and lingering, so you get a concise, great story. The fact that I was in prison was exciting. Plus, the whole journey of playing Nina was such a departure from anything I'd played so far."

From her dramatic, shackled return to CTU to her stone-faced reunion with Bauer in the interrogation room, the episode crackled with energy. "I had the most fun in the second season because I really loved the storyline," Clarke says. She also got to explore new levels of tension with Kiefer. "It's really lucky when you have a story where so many things are unsaid between characters. As long as you trust the energy of the other person, it's all going to translate. We both respected each other enough to let the other do their thing. It's almost like two big cats in a room. I knew that Nina's best tool was what she knew, and I knew to be kind of like a cat, very still. I'm so small physically, I remember thinking it would be so ridiculous to be shackled, like I could really break away from these huge guys," she laughs. "But I also remember thinking I had to puff myself up with confidence. It was the only way I could survive because there really was no way out for Nina."

Research Files

Interrogation Techniques: With his military and CTU background, Jack Bauer is an expert at interrogation techniques, many of which he expends on Nina Myers. There are a variety of effective interrogation techniques including: deception, mental and physical torture, suggestibility, and injection of mind-altering drugs. Controversial, and often officially unsanctioned techniques include: sleep deprivation, exposure to extremes of cold and heat, and placing prisoners in 'stress positions' for long periods of time until they break. In the United States there are legal protections for those being interrogated through legal or military channels, like the right to remain silent and a suspect's right to the presence of a lawyer.

Additional Intel

Sarah Clarke actually learned Arabic for the scenes where she had to communicate with Faheen. She says, "As hard as it was at first, I had a great coach and it gives you a whole other layer and a sense of place and person that you can't fake."

1:00 pm - 2:00 pm

Director: Jon Cassar
Writer: Elizabeth M. Cosin

Guest Cast: Reiko Aylesworth (Michelle Dessler), Skye McCole Bartusiak (Megan Matheson), Innis Casey (Miguel), Sarah Clarke (Nina Myers)

"Don't let anyone in that room and raise the temperature ten degrees." Jack Bauer

Timeframe   Key Events

1:00 P.M. Reporters bombard Palmer about the CTU and helicopter bombings. His ex-wife Sherry Palmer waits for him and asks about the military being evacuated from LA. He assigns Lynne to follow it up.

1:06 P.M. Tony questions Reza who complains about racial profiling.

1:08 P.M. Stanton theorizes about the cause of the helicopter crash. Lynne starts an independent inquiry.

1:09 P.M. Jack steps into the room with Nina, who says she needs to be sent to Visalia to get the location of the bomb. She smugly stands up to Jack and he throws her against the wall and threatens her. Mason orders Jack out of the room, but Jack says it's part of his plan. He asks for five more minutes.

1:21 P.M. Jack shoots at Nina, demanding her contact name. She admits that her contact in Visalia is Mamud Faheen. Mason orders Michelle to call the Visalia authorities.

1:23 P.M. Palmer finds out Stanton ordered the military evacuation. Kim and Miguel see Gary panic about Megan's injuries and ready his family to leave for Mexico.

1:32 P.M. Miguel distracts Gary with a phone call and Kim gets Megan out of the hospital. Kim, Miguel and Megan hide from Gary.

1:35 P.M. Palmer agrees to meet Sherry. She offers help and Palmer tells her of the threat. He agrees to take her help for the sake of the country.

1:43 P.M. Kate greets Reza's parents and they become concerned about the interrogation. Kim and Megan run and are spotted by Gary.

1:47 P.M. Nina is transported and the other agent ignores her small talk.

1:54 P.M. Tony gets Reza to admit transferring money to Syed Ali, but only to cover for Bob Warner — Marie's father. Gary attacks Kim and Miguel knocks Gary out cold with a kick.

1:59 P.M. Jack drugs the other agent, cocks his gun at Nina and smiles.

Sherry Palmer returns.

Jack choke holds Nina.

Tony interrogates Reza.

With Middle Eastern characters as the villains of the season, the producers knew they would have to tread carefully to avoid the inevitable pitfalls of stereotyping that went with that choice. Executive producer Howard Gordon says, "We know the dangers of falling into the easy, cardboard, villain archetype and it's just not as interesting, not only from a political point of view but also from a narrative point of view. It is just more interesting to try and present it in as three-dimensional a way as possible. We recognized that in the real world, as in the fictional world, Muslim allies are going to be a very important part of the fight against Muslim terrorists." With that in mind the character of Reza Naiyeer was crafted to address the new dynamic of Arabs on US soil.

Tony and Reza's heated exchange during this episode hit a number of hot button issues. Actor Carlos Bernard relates, "We were still discovering as a nation how it was that terrorists were recruited and how it wasn't just confined to the Middle Eastern countries. They were going

into Western countries and recruiting students who were impressionable. During the interrogation scene between Reza and I, he accuses me of racial profiling; he tries to use the fact he is a student from England to explain why he shouldn't be suspected. I came up with a version of that scene where I bring up the fact that in real life we were just finding out that one of the biggest recruiting centers for terrorists in the world was this mosque in London. I actually changed the scene with Reza to reflect this and my version ended up being used. Along the way, it was always encouraged that if we had ideas about the scripts, the producers would listen to them. We would play with scenes or change things that didn't make sense to make them work better, but always making sure to check with the writers and the producers on any major changes. That was the first time where I changed an entire major scene, brought it to them and they said, 'Let's do it!'"

Research Files

Presidential Pardon: Nina Myers demands a Presidential Pardon to exonerate her from her sentences for past crimes committed while working as a counter operative against the United States during her employ at CTU. In reality, Presidential Pardons are available through Article II, Section 2 of the US Constitution. All federal pardon petitions are addressed to the President, and are either granted or denied by him. Every year, there are an average of 600 requests for pardons and about ten percent of those are granted. Usually, those pardoned must also admit guilt. A Presidential Pardon may be granted at any time after commission of the offense; the pardoned person may not have been convicted or even formally charged with a crime.

Additional Intel

According to the on-set prop master Sterling Rush, Kiefer Sutherland carries a real, unloaded 9mm H&K compact pistol. Every gun on the show is real, except for rubber guns that are used in stunt scenes.

Kim Bauer

Experience:
Nanny for the Matheson family.

Expertise:
Computers, volleyball, chess

Education:
Santa Monica High School – Dropped out before
matriculation

Personal:
Parents – Jack Bauer and Teri Bauer (deceased)

George Mason

Experience:
CTU – Special Agent in Charge, Los Angeles Domestic Unit
CTU – Senior Section Leader, Washington Headquarters
CTU – Team Leader, Washington Headquarters
CTU – Associate Special Agent in Charge, Phoenix
  Domestic Unit
CTU – Senior Agent, Miami Domestic Unit
CTU – Agent, Los Angeles Domestic Unit

Education:
University of Southern California – Bachelor of Arts,
  Criminal Science

Personal:
Divorced
Son – John Mason

2:00 pm - 3:00 pm

Director: James Whitmore Jr.
Writer: Virgil Williams

Guest Cast: Reiko Aylesworth (Michelle Dessler), Skye McCole Bartusiak (Megan Matheson), Eric Christian Olsen (John Mason)

"What can I say, the guy's a little crazy… But he gets results and we need some pretty big results here." George Mason

Timeframe — Key Events

2:00 P.M. At the airbase, Nina tells the agents Jack drugged an agent.

2:03 P.M. Marie attacks Kate for incriminating Reza. Palmer's Chief of Staff Mike Novick arrives and is shocked to see Sherry. Novick suggests Armus leaks a story about Wieland.

2:08 P.M. Michelle informs Mason of the drugging. Mason finds a radiation rash on his chest. Palmer has Novick investigate Stanton and Rayburn.

2:11 P.M. Jack makes Nina change into civilian clothes in front of him.

2:17 P.M. Mason calls his estranged son to CTU. He refuses to come.

2:19 P.M. The CTU jet lands in Visalia and Nina reveals the location — Crescent Collectibles. Jack takes Nina.

2:22 P.M. Jack wants Nina to prevent Faheen from killing himself to protect the bombing plan.

2:28 P.M. Tony calls Mason with the new suspect, Bob Warner. Mason wants Bob and Reza brought to CTU.

2:33 P.M. Sherry accuses Stanton and Rayburn of working against David. Lynne explains their meetings, but Palmer wants proof Stanton is not against them.

2:38 P.M. Palmer warns Sherry about being competitive with Lynne.

2:42 P.M. Nina enters the store and meets Faheen in the back room. She lies about how she got out of prison. The visuals break up and when Nina hugs Faheen the audio is gone. The SWAT team enters, guns blazing. Faheen is unconscious and Nina has disappeared.

2:51 P.M. Nina tries to escape but Jack catches her. He ponders killing her and slaps cuffs on her.

2:53 P.M. Kim, Miguel and Megan head to Aunt Carol's. The cops pull them over for speeding. LAPD brings in Mason's son. Mason gives him bank account details and tells him he is dying.

2:59 P.M. The police see blood dripping from the trunk. Carla's body is stuffed inside.

Jack pulls a gun on Nina.

Mason says goodbye to John.

Carla's body is in the trunk.

After the success of the first season of *24*, there was a lot of discussion between the network and the producers about how to carry on the concept for the second year. One rumor that circulated amongst fans was that the show intended to abandon the real-time format in year two. Executive producer Howard Gordon confirms it was an option that was discussed, "but we never came close. We entertained the network's request at the time to consider that possibility and actually went as far as writing a script to demonstrate it. I can't say we put a lot of elbow grease into that script so that helped make the case that this is what the show is, and this is what it will always be, and fortunately they agreed." Kiefer Sutherland concurs, "We had such an amazing audience who were supporting us on a strong level, and we had members of the press who were supporting us on a strong level. To take advantage of all of that for the first season and then kind of turn it on them might have meant the end of the

show — it would have certainly hurt the trust that we had built from the first season. I think to walk away from what made the show so special, which was the time element, would have been disastrous. I think the network realized that very quickly too."

Another curious aspect of the show is the lack of screen time given to Jack Bauer actually doing human things like eating, dozing or even using the men's room. While there was a fleeting moment of sleep — a split second of vulnerability for Jack in season one — he's been superhuman since. Executive producer Evan Katz laughs saying, "Jack's a hero: he doesn't eat. We tried eating during the first season." Sutherland agrees revealing, "Every year I've eaten at least once and Joel Surnow has cut it out. I even used the bathroom once and he cut that out. And I have fallen asleep too, in every season. I have even been sitting on surveillance in a car and fallen asleep: he cut that out. We've tried!"

Research Files

Visalia: Nina Myers requires that Bauer and CTU take her to Visalia, California, to speak to her contact in person. The town of Visalia is the county seat of Tulare County, California. With a population of more that 100,000, Visalia is one of the largest inland cities in the state of California and one of the largest in between Fresno and Bakersfield. Founded in 1852 by Nathaniel Vise, Visalia is the oldest city between Stockton and Los Angeles. The town has a commercial airport with multiple daily flights to Los Angeles International.

Additional Intel

In this episode, George Mason gives his son access to a special account containing $200,000. In season one, Jack accused Mason of skimming that amount of money from a CTU operation — making it the likely source of Mason's hidden money.

3:00 pm - 4:00 pm

Director: James Whitmore Jr.
Writers: Joel Surnow & Michael Loceff

Guest Cast: Skye McCole Bartusiak (Megan Matheson), Jude Ciccolella (Mike Novick), Phillip Rhys (Reza Naiyeer), Sarah Clarke (Nina Myers)

"Well, she's his ex-wife. That's a problem all by itself." Roger Stanton

Timeframe

Key Events

3:00 P.M. The cops arrest Miguel and Kim. Tony escorts Reza and Bob into CTU.

3:03 P.M. Stanton inquires about Sherry's provisional clearance. Kim begs the cop not to take Megan back to LA.

3:08 P.M. Nina tries to get information out of Faheen. Jack gets impatient and grabs Nina. The agents won't let Jack be alone with her.

3:14 P.M. Paul Koplin, Kate's investigator's boss, tells Kate he knows about the files that link Reza to Syed Ali. He attaches a transmitter to Bob's computer.

3:18 P.M. The van with the bomb gets a flat tire.

3:20 P.M. On the CTU jet, Nina persuades Faheen to talk. He calls her a traitor. Nina hides a piece of gift card in her hand.

3:29 P.M. Sherry talks to Palmer about regaining his confidence.

3:31 P.M. One of the van drivers panics and two of the men shoot each other.

3:37 P.M. Koplin uncovers government files on Bob's database, which need security clearance to be read. Kate is confused.

3:40 P.M. Tony gets Bob to admit he is working as a consultant for the CIA.

3:43 P.M. Michelle patches Kim through to Jack and tells him she is falsely accused of murder. Nina and Faheen talk quietly. Nina gets Faheen's secrets then slits his throat with the gift card. Nina demands the plane go to San Diego and she will reveal the plan. Mason agrees.

3:51 P.M. Michelle tells Mason she picked up the conversation and connected the name Marko Khatami to Syed Ali. Mason attacks Reza accusing him of knowing Khatami. Reza denies this. Tony pulls Mason off Reza and Marie goes to Reza's aid. The officer tells Kim and Miguel they are going to CTU. Kim reveals the bomb threat.

3:56 P.M. Two men appear in the Warner yard, attack Kate and Koplin and take them.

3:59 P.M. An explosion rocks the CTU plane.

The terrorists turn on each other.

Nina slits Faheen's throat.

An explosion rocks the CTU plane.

The tension-filled sequence in the CTU plane, leading to Nina's brutal killing of Faheen, remains one of Sarah Clarke's favorite moments in the second season: "I loved the airplane scene! The sequence where I killed Faheen with the gift card was so complicated. I remember the actor playing my bodyguard on the plane marveling, because, at one point, we have the conversation going on between Jack and his daughter and Mason; then we have my Arabic going on with Faheen. There was no way for the director to cue us because I was supposed to be saying things that are being translated, so everyone had to be doing this weird listening. Meanwhile, Faheen has no idea what is being said. I'm shackled and I had to lean down and tap his knee to cue him to get really upset. I remember my bodyguard was going, 'Whoa, there's all this communication going on and I have no idea what's happening!'

"Those scenes in particular are when Kiefer is really good. What I loved playing in Nina was when Jack would get really mad and I would get even more liquid and pay it blasé, and it would just get him even angrier," she laughs.

Knowing the Nina arc would be quite potent, executive producer Howard Gordon admits bringing her back was more of an idea than a plan. "The details of how we brought her back weren't as organic as the need to bring her back, because she was clearly a piece of unfinished business for Jack. The challenge though was finding a really good way to dispatch her. Jack killing her in cold blood, which he did in an early draft of the script, didn't feel satisfying. For the resolution in the second season there was no good way to do it, so we had Jack whisper this cryptic thing, and no one ever knew what he said... apart from Kiefer."

Research Files

ASCII Code: Paul Koplin and Kate Warner try to sift through Bob Warner's files and find many of them are government related and coded in ASCII. Since computers can only understand numbers, American Standard Code for Information Interchange (ASCII) is a character-encoding system based on the English alphabet, first published as a standard in 1967 and last updated in 1986. In an ASCII file, each of the 128 alphabetic, numeric and special characters is represented by a seven digit binary number (a string of seven 0s or 1s) from zero to 127. There is also the Extended ASCII Character Set — representing additional special, mathematical, graphic, and foreign characters — which consists of 128 decimal numbers, from 128 through 255.

Additional Intel

During the first season of *24*, actors Xander Berkeley and Sarah Clarke began secretly dating. When the couple got engaged the following year, Sarah Clarke made the announcement to the entire production crew of 200 that she was "marrying George!"

4:00 pm - 5:00 pm

Director: Rodney Charters
Writer: Howard Gordon

Guest Cast: Reiko Aylesworth (Michelle Dessler), Skye McCole Bartusiak (Megan Matheson), Al Sapienza (Paul Koplin), Sarah Clarke (Nina Myers)

"This isn't over yet." Jack Bauer (to Nina Myers)

Timeframe — Key Events

4:00 P.M. Wieland is released and Palmer blames Sherry. Palmer realizes Armus let him go. The CTU jet is crashing. Jack begs Nina for the bomb location. Jack relays the situation to Mason.

4:06 P.M. Palmer wants Armus. Novick tells Palmer Jack's plane crashed.

4:08 P.M. Jack survives with a branch in his thigh and he performs CPR on Nina.

4:16 P.M. Michelle shows Mason that a missile shot down Jack's plane. Mason's health is failing.

4:19 P.M. Kim and Miguel are sent to central booking in LA. Kim says her father will fix things.

4:28 P.M. Michelle admits to Tony that she knows Mason has radiation poisoning.

4:30 P.M. Sherry gives speech revisions to Lynne, which incenses the aide.

4:33 P.M. Hostile soldiers arrive and Jack grabs Nina. Gunshots are exchanged and Jack orders Nina to run reconnaissance while he shoots. Kate and Paul are awakened by Syed Ali. He wants details about the files found in Bob's computer.

4:40 P.M. Nina slips an extra clip in her pocket. A CTU helicopter appears overhead and fires at the soldiers. Nina grabs Jack's gun, loads the clip and orders Jack to drop his gun. She demands to speak to President Palmer.

4:43 P.M. Megan heads to her aunt's in Santa Barbara, and Kim is grateful for her safety.

4:45 P.M. Reza tells Marie that Bob set him up.

4:52 P.M. Nina wants full immunity for the murder of Jack Bauer. Jack tells Mason they must accept the deal. Palmer agrees if the information successfully allows them to intercept the bomb. Nina reveals Syed is in Chatsworth.

4:57 P.M. Palmer commends Lynne on improving his speech as Sherry listens.

4:59 P.M. Ali kills Paul and orders Kate must die next. Nina tells Jack the end is near.

Megan says goodbye to Kim.

Reza tells Marie that Bob has set him up.

Paul is killed.

Special effects coordinators Stan and Scott Blackwell are the men behind all the complicated gunfights staged during the series. When a round is shot or a bullet hits someone, it's the Blackwell brothers who make it look realistic. For *24*, Stan explains they are often asked to do those signature standoff moments with Jack Bauer facing down the barrel of the bad guy's gun. "The unique thing about this show is that when there is a shootout or someone gets shot, they'll often actually show the bullets hitting in the same shot. It's me pulling the trigger to set off the squibs on the guy, so there's a real timing issue between me and the actor: we have to be in synch. Kiefer is great at it. We get a sight on him and go off his finger, as he is pulling the trigger. But sometimes when you have someone who isn't very savvy with weapons, it gets interesting." He relates that one of those times was during the tense standoff between Nina and Jack after the plane crash. "Nina has the automatic weapon and she says she will kill him. Jack

says, 'I'm already dead' and walks away, so she shoots the bushes next to him. So I set up a bunch of hits in the bushes and afterwards Kiefer goes to me, 'Nice timing, Stan' and Sarah just looked at me and said, 'Nice timing on what?' I said, 'That was me setting off those hits in the bushes.' I think she thought for a minute she had a real weapon and had done it herself! But I wasn't giving her a machine gun when she had never shot a gun before!" he laughs.

For her part, Clarke says she got her biggest injuries during Nina's takedown. "It was a very rocky terrain and I had absolutely no padding on. We didn't know how it was going to go down, and we didn't even really talk it through, but I knew it was going to be violent. When I got shot and had to scramble for the gun, it was all adrenaline. We did one take and I was like, 'Ow, my knee!' I remember by the third time, I was saying, 'I can't do it again unless I get padding!'" she laughs.

Research Files

Chatsworth: After the plane crashes, Nina Myers gets immunity for her intended murder of Jack Bauer and reveals that Ali's safe house is in Chatsworth, California. Situated in the northwest San Fernando Valley, Chatsworth is a community of Los Angeles, bordered by the Santa Susana Mountains. Chatsworth is known for its rural look, and has been home to many famous people, including Roy Rogers; and the infamous, such as Charles Manson and his 'family'. The town is named for Chatsworth House, the ancestral home of the Dukes of Devonshire in England. In reality, Chatsworth is also home to the *24* shooting stages and production offices.

Additional Intel

Native New Zealander and *24* director of photography Rodney Charters made his directorial début on the show with this and the following episode. He had previously directed installments of *Hercules*, *The Pretender* and *Roswell*.

5:00 pm - 6:00 pm

Director: Rodney Charters
Writer: David Ehrman

Guest Cast: Jude Ciccolella (Mike Novick), Laura Harris (Marie Warner), Daniel Dae Kim (Agent Tom Baker), Sarah Clarke (Nina Myers)

"What are we saying here? If we save LA from a nuclear bomb, you and I can get together for dinner and a movie?" Tony Almeida

Timeframe

Key Events

5:00 P.M. Palmer admits there is a terror threat, but there is no cause for alarm. A sharpshooter gets Nina in the hand. CTU agents converge and Jack is saved.

5:04 P.M. Kim and Miguel fight being taken back to LA. Novick tells Palmer that Nina was taken down and is alive. Jack whispers something to Nina and she looks fearful.

5:08 P.M. Kate is tortured.

5:14 P.M. Jack calls Palmer to tell him the soldiers that attacked his plane were American, from an NSA undercover special ops unit. Palmer asks Stanton about the Coral Snake Unit and he denies knowledge. Palmer distrusts Stanton and orders Novick to find a connection between him and the unit's commander, Colonel Samuels.

5:21 P.M. Miguel and Kim light a fire in the cop car and it topples into an embankment.

5:28 P.M. Kim crawls out and calls dispatch for help.

5:32 P.M. Jack and the team enter Ali's house and shoot Kate's torturer. Jack orders an analysis to prove the torturer was Ali.

5:39 P.M. Kim goes on the run. Kate tells Jack that Ali escaped and describes what he looks like.

5:43 P.M. Jack calls Tony about the Warner family connection to the bomb threat.

5:46 P.M. Sherry discovers a secret OPCOM channel Stanton restarted a month ago that might connect him to the special ops team. Palmer is grateful.

5:54 P.M. Kate relates the torture session for Jack and says she heard them say "prayer". Jack takes Kate to a mosque to look for Ali.

5:56 P.M. Sherry calls Stanton and tells him her plan to get back into Palmer's confidence is working and warns him not to reveal the plan when he is arrested.

5:58 P.M. Reza finds evidence of a hacker on the computer. Marie shoots him dead.

Nina is taken down by a sharpshooter.

The cop car carrying Kim and Miguel crashes.

Marie shoots Reza dead.

Over the course of the season, a romantic relationship bloomed between CTU agents Tony Almeida and Michelle Dessler. According to director Jon Cassar, that storyline evolved out of sheer chemistry and happenstance on the set. "The Michelle piece was born out of my blocking, and those first scenes Reiko had with Carlos. There was never any intention of them being a couple — never. She was just the worker of the year: every year, we bring in a new CTU person and she was it. But the very first scene they had together, there was something that I saw right away. There was a neat little magic between the two actors, and they looked good together. I blocked a scene where they had to both go behind a table at the same time, and there was a moment where they just stopped and kind of looked at each other, and then walked away. It wasn't in the script; it was just something we did and from that the writers looked at their relationship. In another scene, when CTU blew up, Tony was all upset and she was about to touch

him — again, not something in the script."

For Carlos Bernard, getting to craft a romance set against the CTU chaos was a highlight of the season. "It was fun developing the Michelle and Tony relationship. It was interesting trying to cultivate it in a believable way over the course of one day. The thing about trying to build an arc for a character over one single day is that it's like walking a fine line. It got to the point with the writers where they almost handed the scenes over to Reiko, Jon Cassar and myself to really get down to the specifics of shaping them. They would write scenes for us that on the page maybe worked, but when you got it on stage, it was maybe heavy-handed or not quite subtle enough. Again, you can't give them enough credit because they really were able to hand it over to us to cut and shape to make it work a little bit better. The three of us really worked together through that season, and the rest of the run, to make those scenes believable."

Research Files

Infrared Imaging: To plan their mode of entry, CTU agents scan Ali's safe house with infrared imaging to determine how many people are inside. Infrared is heat radiation emitted by anything with a temperature above 'absolute zero' (-459.67°F). The higher an object's temperature is, the more infrared radiation it emits. All objects emit a certain amount of this heat radiation, and while the human eye can't see it, thermographic cameras can detect it (almost as a standard camera does visible light). Originally developed for military use during the Korean War, thermographic cameras have slowly migrated into other fields. When looking at infrared imaging, the red areas of the picture are the warmest, followed by yellow, then green, with the coolest being blue.

Additional Intel

Kiefer Sutherland sustained an injury to his knee during season two when he fell coming out of his trailer. Producers wrote in a scene where he pulls out a piece of shrapnel from his leg after the plane crash to explain his limp.

6:00 pm - 7:00 pm

Director: Frederick K. Keller
Writer: Gil Grant

Guest Cast: Reiko Aylesworth (Michelle Dessler), Michelle Forbes (Lynne Kresge), Michael James Reed (Foreman), Edward Edwards (Colonel Lamb)

"You're not a member of my staff, you're not a government employee and you're not my wife."
President David Palmer

Timeframe	Key Events

6:00 P.M. Kim escapes into the forest. Marie guts her father's hard drive. Ali calls and tells Marie she needs to get the bomb trigger and take it to the van.
6:05 P.M. Jack tells Kate about the bomb threat. Mason calls Jack about Kim's accident. Jack begs Mason to find her.
6:08 P.M. Novick tells Palmer there isn't enough evidence against Stanton, but he should be relieved.
6:10 P.M. Kate offers to enter the mosque wearing a hijab to look for Ali.
6:16 P.M. Stanton is arrested for treason. Sherry calls to disagree with Palmer, but he refuses to listen to her.
6:20 P.M. Tony and Michelle discuss their new relationship. There is a commotion in the interrogation room as Bob Warner demands to be freed as he believes Reza is lying about his involvement with the terrorists. Tony orders him to stay calm. When Bob asks about his daughters, Tony tells him that Kate is with one of their agents but doesn't tell him what is happening. Kate is prepped to enter the mosque.
6:24 P.M. Kate spots Ali inside and tells Jack as she exits.
6:30 P.M. Palmer offers Stanton immunity for information about the bomb threat. Stanton denies all wrongdoing.
6:33 P.M. Jack thanks Kate for her help and the team preps to apprehend Ali. A cougar in the woods stalks Kim.
6:41 P.M. Palmer orders former covert CIA op Simmons to get the truth from Stanton by any means possible. Michelle gets word about Reza's murder and she alerts Jack that Marie is a suspect.
6:53 P.M. Palmer watches Simmons torture Stanton.
6:54 P.M. Tony informs Bob Warner about Reza's murder and the suspicion of Marie as the killer. Bob accuses Tony of trying to trick him.
6:56 P.M. Jack's team raids the mosque and finds a man inside engulfed in flames. Marie retrieves the trigger at a mill.
6:59 P.M. The flaming man is made to look like Ali, but Jack realizes it isn't and he's still on the loose.

Kim identifies Ali in the mosque.

A cougar in the woods stalks Kim.

A flaming man acts as a decoy for Ali.

The much-lamented cougar storyline lives in infamy as one of the least successful uses of Kim Bauer in the show. Joel Surnow readily admits it wasn't their finest moment, but he details the context of the story's development. "We wanted to keep Kim in play, because we love Elisha. We struggled so much with Kim that season because we didn't have an organic place for her to be. Every story needs a suspenseful element to it, and so we put her in a domestic suspense thriller. We took her out of the house and it meandered about and ended up with the infamous cougar chasing her." Critics were merciless, and Surnow says candidly, "We probably deserved it. I mean it was one shot and it sort of became legendary by the time we got done. We freely admitted to ourselves that it was probably not the best thing for our show to have characters who are not involved in the main terrorist plotline.

"We learned our lesson after the second season by not creating characters who are just point of view characters, who run through the season and are not involved in the main play. That's why we brought Elisha into CTU in season three."

For her part, Elisha Cuthbert says the storyline marked a change for her too. "I knew the complications of what was happening that year, and that they were struggling. I learned that year that I had the opportunity to speak up for myself and say, 'Guys, I'm trying to make this work for you every week, and it's difficult.' It set the tone for how I felt as an actor, I was allowed to step in and say, 'Hey guys, I want this to change' or 'I have ideas.' Season two really got me to communicate, not just what I wanted to do with the script but with the producers and the writers and everyone involved."

Research Files

Hijab: Kate Warner offers to don a hijab to enter the mosque to look for Ali. A hijab comes from the Arabic term 'hijaba' which means to hide from view. In Muslim culture, it is the long dress and veil worn by women to conceal their person from the view of someone of the opposite sex other than a close family member. The rules surrounding the use of hijab are often dictated by each particular culture and by traditions laid out by Muslim families. Most scholars agree that the rules of hijab can be waived if following them would result in risk of death or extreme hardship. In countries like Saudi Arabia and Iran, women must wear the national version of Islamic dress or face punishment by religious police.

Additional Intel

Elisha Cuthbert was actually bitten on the hand by the trained cougar that stalks her in the episode. She was treated in the hospital for puncture wounds, given a tetanus shot, and returned to work shortly afterwards.

7:00 pm – 8:00 pm

Director: Frederick K. Keller
Writer: Evan Katz

Guest Cast: Jude Ciccolella (Mike Novick), Francesco Quinn (Syed Ali), Kevin Dillon (Lonnie McRae), Bernard White (Imam Al Fulani)

> "The only way you're gonna die today is if I kill ya." Jack Bauer

Timeframe — Key Events

7:00 P.M. Jack's team finds a trap door in the mosque and enters.

7:04 P.M. In the basement, Ali calls Marie. Jack apprehends Ali and takes the cyanide capsule from his teeth.

7:06 P.M. Mason tells Bob Warner that Marie is working for Ali.

7:09 P.M. Novick tells Palmer of Ali's capture. Palmer waits for Stanton to break.

7:14 P.M. Tony organizes a rescue effort for Kim despite Mason's protests.

7:17 P.M. Jack interrogates Ali.

7:20 P.M. Jack finds Ali's cell phone and Marie's number comes up. Kate is shocked and Jack tells her about Reza's murder.

7:28 P.M. The techs rig a call from Kate to Marie and they are able to trace the call to an area in Sylmar before Marie throws her phone out of the car.

7:31 P.M. Michelle investigates the handwritten 'N34' on the charred paper found on the burnt man. Jack presses Ali for bomb details and he refuses. On a satellite video feed, Jack shows Ali his wife and children.

7:39 P.M. Jack threatens to kill Ali's family, but Palmer calls and forbids Jack to kill innocent people. Jack pretends that Palmer backs him.

7:43 P.M. Lynne tells Novick that Sherry is untrustworthy. She reveals Sherry has been communicating with Stanton for six months. Novick holds off telling Palmer.

7:45 P.M. Jack orders Ali's son to be killed and Ali watches in horror via the satellite, but still does not talk.

7:51 P.M. Jack is about to order the next murder when Ali breaks. He reveals the plan is to detonate the bomb from a plane over downtown. The bomb is at Norton Airfield. Teams are dispatched.

7:57 P.M. Jack reveals to Kate the killing was staged and takes her to Norton with him.

7:59 P.M. Marie arrives at a hangar and connects the trigger to the bomb.

Jack apprehends Ali.

Jack orders Ali's son to be killed.

Marie connects the trigger to the bomb.

Due to the shifting storylines and extremely tight turnaround from script to production on *24*, casting is often one of the more challenging departments to work in on the show. Casting director Debi Manwiller details, "We don't have any advance notice with the scripts, we get them not that far from actual production. But at the beginning of the year, the producers come in and tell us where the season is going to start and what the early storyline is." For season two, the producers did know that the role of Marie Warner would be more complicated than just that of a happy young bride-to-be. "We talked about Marie Warner early on and we knew that much further down the season she was going to turn bad. We didn't know how and we didn't know why, but we knew she was going to have to take this big turn.

"They wanted us to keep it a secret, so we didn't tell the

actors. We just knew we had to have an actress who would be able to serve up something like that further down the line, so they were mindful of that, as were we, when we were looking for someone to play Marie. We kept that reveal a total secret — they didn't even tell Laura Harris, who played Marie, until the script came out! For an actor, what's great about it is that as she didn't know in advance, she couldn't play any of that. Sometimes too much information is a bad thing. It's different when you are doing a two-hour movie, you know how it ends, but this is all season long. I think it's good the actors don't have that information beforehand as it would inform their performance in an unconscious way, and it would be hard to keep a lid on that. You would always be thinking about trying to hide what you know. If you don't know, you play it at face value."

Research Files

Cyanide Capsules: The terrorists are provided with cyanide capsules in their teeth to bite down on if they are captured and need to circumvent being tortured for information. Cyanide capsules or poison pills have been used throughout history to incur fast-acting suicide. There are stories of spy agents who carried spectacles with cyanide in the frames. If caught by the enemy, the option was to casually chew the frame, releasing the cyanide into their system, so they could die before being tortured or having information extracted from them. Infamous people who ingested cyanide to hasten their deaths include Adolf Hitler, Erwin Rommel, Heinrich Himmler and the Jonestown Mass Suicide victims.

Additional Intel

Veteran character actor Harris Yulin appeared in eleven episodes as the treacherous Roger Stanton, yet the actor chose to remain uncredited for the season. He previously worked with Joel Surnow and Robert Cochran on *La Femme Nikita*.

Tony Almeida

CTU Missions:
Operation Proteus, 2000 (Special Commendation)

Experience:
CTU – Intelligence Agent, Los Angeles Domestic Unit
Transmeta Corporation – Systems Validation Analyst

Expertise:
Certified Instructor, Krav Maga hand-to-hand
  combat defense

Education:
Stanford University – Masters of Science, Computer
  Science
San Diego State University – Combined Bachelor of
  Engineering/Bachelor of Computer Science

Military:
US Marines – First Lieutenant
Scout-Sniper School (3rd Marine Division)
Surveillance & Target Acquisition Platoon School (1st
  Marine Division)

Personal:
Single

Michelle Dessler

Experience:

CTU – Internet Protocol Manager, Los Angeles
    Domestic Unit
DARPA – High Confidence Systems Working Group
National Institute of Standards & Technology –
    Computer Security Division

Expertise:

Built IPSec architecture.
Attacks scripts, computer vulnerabilities, intrusion
    detection, penetration testing, operational security,
    viruses.
Proficiency in Cerberus and PlutoPlus.

Education:

University of California (Davis) – Bachelor of Science,
    Computer Science

Personal:

Single

8:00 pm - 9:00 pm

Director: Jon Cassar
Writer: Maurice Hurley

Guest Cast: Reiko Aylesworth (Michelle Dessler), Michelle Forbes (Lynne Kresge), Randle Mell (Brad Hammond), Kevin Dillon (Lonnie McRae)

"Sherry. She's the one you want to talk to."
Roger Stanton

Timeframe	Key Events

8:00 P.M. Jack calls Tony about Kim. In the woods, a man named McRae helps the injured Kim to his cabin.

8:03 P.M. Stanton admits to Palmer he is part of a group that wants to make Palmer's defense policy more aggressive. They allowed Second Wave to operate, but Colonel Samuels has been monitoring the bomb, so it won't detonate.

8:06 P.M. Mason sends all agents to Norton Airfield. Mason calls Jack about the Coral Unit.

8:09 P.M. Marie and the pilot Omar see police cars on the airfield. Jack and Kate arrive and Jack briefs the assembled assault squads.

8:16 P.M. Division wants to shut down Mason's CTU unit. Kim tells McRae about the bomb threat and he isn't shocked. Palmer allows Sherry access to the secure databases, despite protests.

8:22 P.M. Jack and SWAT raid the fuel depot and find the Coral Snake commandos have all been executed.

8:28 P.M. Mason is failing and Brad Hammond from Division orders resources sent to the operational center.

8:30 P.M. McRae shows Kim his bomb shelter.

8:33 P.M. Lynne gives Sherry her access cards but demands Sherry not deal with personnel but run everything through her.

8:40 P.M. McRae covers for Kim when a park ranger comes looking for her. She explains the charges are false.

8:43 P.M. A livid Palmer tells Stanton of the six dead Coral Unit members. Stanton is shocked and says there were seven soldiers in the team. The bombing plane is in hangar MD7. Jack sees Marie and Omar prepare to take off. They shoot Omar and stop the plane.

8:52 P.M. The team realizes the bomb is a decoy.

8:55 P.M. McRae convinces Kim the bomb went off and despite her pleas to find her dad, they go into the bomb shelter.

8:59 P.M. Palmer confronts Stanton again, who tells the President to talk to Sherry.

The Coral Snake commandos are all murdered.

Jack attacks the plane.

McRae convinces Kim the bomb went off.

After directing two episodes in season one, Jon Cassar took on the role of primary director for season two and was responsible for ten episodes. "In the second year, Stephen Hopkins decided to move on and they offered me the job. It meant a life change for me because I was living in Toronto at the time with my family, and I knew I didn't want to do it long-distance. Luckily, my family wanted the adventure."

Cassar says shooting *24* was a whole different world from the TV norm. "Stephen didn't have a background in television, he was a feature guy. He changed everything all the time, which you have the ability to do in features. He came in to *24* and threw things away, charged it up, made it all live and never stopped moving the camera. He let the actors do whatever they wanted to do and followed them. He saw a scene that was a little static and opened it up. As a director, I analyzed the shows. I'm a homework

guy and before I read my first script here, I saw every episode they ever shot. I was able to break it down and I got how they were doing it. Partly because I was a camera operator for so many years, it was very easy for me to let the camera go. While others might have been very intimidated by the style, I took to it right away.

"I also built up a really good relationship with Kiefer almost instantly, and that's a big part of a successful television show, the way the personalities meld together," Cassar continues. "Kiefer and I were just in the same headspace right away. We both have the same work ethic. The bottom line for both of us is only one thing — a really good show. We don't really care about anything else. But for me, as a director, artistically, it's been a real challenge. It's a very difficult show to do. It never gets easier, rather it gets harder and that's why the show is so good — because it gets harder every year. Nobody is ready to sit back and say, 'Oh, we've done this before, let's do it the same.' Nobody in any department is doing that."

Research Files

UV Light: The investigations team uses UV light to collect clues and samples. Ultra violet light has become an important alternative scene-of-crime light source in forensic investigation. Besides latent fingerprints and footprints, a high intensity UV light source increases the probability of detecting certain types of matter. For example, it is extremely effective in showing up dust, hair, seeds, and innumerable other items clinging unseen to a person or object. Scar tissue on flesh and natural teeth glow a bright pearlish white under UV light (false teeth glow green, or not at all). Stains, secretions, lipstick, inks, and foreign matter become visible with UV, even after cleaning or drying.

Additional Intel

Traditionally each episode of *24* ends with a ticking clock. Starting with Teri Bauer's death, the producers decided to denote a significant character loss with a silent clock sequence. The second time this occurred was in this episode, as George Mason made his final exit from CTU (although he wouldn't actually die for another two hours).

9:00 pm - 10:00 pm

Director: Jon Cassar
Writers: Joel Surnow & Michael Loceff

Guest Cast: Reiko Aylesworth (Michelle Dessler),
Laura Harris (Marie Warner), John Terry (Bob
Warner), Lourdes Benedicto (Carrie Turner)

"Wake up Marie! You're about to become the
biggest murderer in the history of this country."
Kate Warner

Timeframe	Key Events

9:00 P.M. Jack needs a translator to talk to Omar. Mason is failing badly, but tells Jack the seventh member of the team is missing. Kate calls Bob to tell him Marie is a terrorist. Jack asks Kate to help him with Omar.

9:04 P.M. Palmer summons Sherry and asks her to come clean. She admits Stanton approached her and she did it to protect him.

9:09 P.M. Through Kate and a translator they establish Omar knows nothing. Kate spots a disguised Marie in another part of the airfield.

9:15 P.M. In the bomb shelter, McRae tells Kim that all radio contact with LA has been lost. Carrie Turner, the new programmer, arrives and reports to Mason.

9:19 P.M. Kate follows Marie and is stunned when her sister pulls a gun and demands her ID badge. The women squabble and Jack shoots Marie in the arm.

9:28 P.M. Jack leaves the bullet in her arm and says they will remove it when she reveals the other bomb location. She refuses.

9:31 P.M. After finding a TV with LA stations broadcasting normally, Kim realizes that she is in danger from McRae.

9:33 P.M. Tony finds out the seventh commando in the Coral Snake Unit is Jonathan Wallace. Mason names Tony the new Director and leaves.

9:42 P.M. Jack gives Marie a painkiller and she relents, telling him the bomb is in a suitcase being transported by a green van to the Arco Towers downtown. It will detonate in three hours. Jack doesn't believe Marie and orders another hangar search.

9:52 P.M. Unsure of Sherry's stories and lies, Palmer orders her to leave and threatens her with arrest. Kim battles with McRae and he lets her go.

9:59 P.M. Jack finds the actual nuclear bomb at the airfield. It is armed and could blow any second.

Marie is interrogated.

Mason names Tony the new Director.

Jack finds the nuclear bomb.

Despite the meltdown of the Palmer marriage at the end of season one, producers knew Sherry Palmer would be a powerful character to bring back somewhere during the life of the series. "We didn't know if we wanted her to be around for another season, but we try not to kill people off for the sake of killing them off," executive producer Howard Gordon points out. "It's better to have them possibly come back another day, and if it's not going to be a good and meaningful end we try to forestall it."

Sherry's still breathing status resulted in a reunion with David during season two. The estranged couple shared an uneasy alliance throughout the day, culminating in a new bout of Sherry's duplicitous machinations. Gordon admits creating the story was a huge challenge. "To an extent, David Palmer was unconsciously complicit in what she had done. There is an

interesting moment where she looks at him and says, basically, 'You needed me and you got to this place because of me — you know it. I protected you and your hands were clean because of me.' These weren't just the rantings of a psychotic woman, there is a part of her that David Palmer knew was speaking the truth. Plus, she still loved him and believed in him and she understood that, as a leader, it was necessary for him to do certain things to make sure he maintained his power. We got to play all that stuff; and even once all cards were on the table, there was still a lot more to play between them. Their story was definitely not over yet, and that part was great. The drama becomes more intense and subtle and nuanced than before."

Research Files

Fallout Shelters: Kim's mountain-man protector, McRae, shows the teenager the fallout shelter he's built in his remote cabin, stocked with enough guns, ammunition and food to survive a nuclear explosion. Fallout shelters came into being at the height of the Cold War in the 1950s. They are a civil defense measure intended to reduce casualties in a nuclear war. Many countries built fallout shelters for high-ranking government officials and crucial military facilities. A basic fallout shelter consists of shields that reduce gamma ray exposure by a factor of 1000. According to standards set by the Federal Emergency Management Agency, a minimum of three cubic feet of fresh air per minute per fallout shelter occupant shall be provided to prevent oxygen depletion and carbon dioxide buildup.

Additional Intel

The Palmer Cabinet boards Air Force One, which was a set that was actually built for the film *Air Force One*, starring Harrison Ford. Coincidentally, a large contingent of *24* actors, including Wendy Crewson, Xander Berkeley, Bill Smitrovich, Glenn Morshower, Mark Thompson, J. Scott Shonka and Timothy Carhart, had also appeared in that film.

10:00 pm - 11:00 pm

Director: Ian Toynton
Writer: Robert Cochran

Guest Cast: Jude Ciccolella (Mike Novick), Michelle Forbes (Lynne Kresge), Maximilian Martini (Agent Steve Goodrich), Neal Matarazzo (Agent Graves)

"You get back down there and you put the pieces together. Find a way to forgive yourself for what happened to your wife, you make things right with your daughter, and you go on serving your country." George Mason

Timeframe — Key Events

10:00 P.M. N.E.S.T. attempts to diffuse the bomb, but it is tamper proof. Mason arrives at the airbase to see the case through to the end. There are fifty-five minutes until detonation.

10:05 P.M. Kim walks along a deserted road. Jack and Palmer discuss where to take the bomb: the ocean or the desert. Palmer's team decides the desert is best, but it will be a suicide mission.

10:11 P.M. Mason offers to take the mission since he's dying already. Jack refuses.

10:19 P.M. Jack calls Tony and says he needs to find Kim since he is going on the suicide mission.

10:21 P.M. Kim is picked up by a woman who lets her call Jack on her cell. Kate is horrified that Jack is flying the mission.

10:28 P.M. Palmer wants Air Force One to take him back to Los Angeles. He is shocked to hear Jack will be the pilot.

10:31 P.M. Tony patches Kim through to Jack and the two exchange a sorrowful goodbye.

10:39 P.M. Kim runs off into the night. Michelle establishes from recorded conversations on Ali's hard drive that three Middle Eastern governments supplied the bomb. Tony alerts the President.

10:43 P.M. On the plane, Jack is surprised when Mason appears. He hands Jack a parachute and says he can take over the mission now. Jack instructs him where to crash and thanks Mason.

10:52 P.M. Jack phones Tony about the change of plans.

10:54 P.M. General Bowden from the Joint Chiefs comes in to see Palmer to discuss retaliation. The President now sees imminent war brewing.

10:57 P.M. Jack and Mason shake hands and then Jack leaps to safety.

10:59 P.M. A mushroom cloud grows over the desert.

Jack and Kim say goodbye by phone.

Mason takes over the mission.

The bomb detonates.

A prolific character actor, primarily in film before *24*, actor Xander Berkeley says that despite his love of the series, he knew it was time to move on from George Mason by year two: "The producers knew that I had this perverse apprehension about getting overly identified with one character. It's my thing to play lots of different characters. An actor's efficacy is so fragile, and nowhere more so than on TV can it be obliterated permanently because people identify you with one guy. I felt like I could do one more season and get away with it." Thus, the demise of Mason worked out creatively all around. "We figured it out ahead of time. They said they had a great story for me and would be able to turn my character around, and kill me, by the end of it, by establishing that I inhale airborne plutonium. With my hours numbered, it would create great drama and intensity for the show and we could show sides of Mason that weren't revealed before;

he shows remorse for having led a life misspent in many ways. It sounded fantastic, I couldn't have been happier, and we were all on the same page to start the second season."

Mason's journey to his heroic death, detonating the nuclear bomb in Jack's stead, was deeply satisfying for the actor, though a bit more accelerated than expected. "They kind of surprised me with the speed with which they moved the story. They were getting a little tired of the bomb storyline and they needed to get rid of the bomb before it bombed," he laughs. "So they thought they had to take advantage of getting rid of the bomb to get rid of Mason, because it made him into the ultimate hero and it kept him from slowly, morbidly dropping an ear and an arm. When I read that episode, it was the one episode I didn't change a word in because it was just perfect; it was flawless."

Research Files

Air Force One: President Palmer takes Air Force One back to Los Angeles. Air Force One is the air traffic control call sign of any US Air Force aircraft carrying the President of the United States. It is a common misconception that Air Force One refers to a single plane. The first president to fly in an airplane while in office was Franklin D. Roosevelt in 1943. The call sign was established for security purposes during the administration of Dwight D. Eisenhower (1953-1961) after a commercial plane and the President's plane were given the same call sign and entered the same air space. Air Force One was created to deter that happening again and has been used ever since.

Additional Intel

When they were filming the scene in which Kim and Jack say their tearful goodbye on the phone, Elisha Cuthbert reveals she was in the front seat of the car, while Kiefer was laying in the back seat saying the off-camera lines. When he was in the plane, Elisha was in the seat behind him.

11:00 pm - 12:00 am

Director: Ian Toynton
Writers: Howard Gordon & Evan Katz

Guest Cast: Daniel Dae Kim (Agent Tom Baker), Donnie Keshawarz (Yusuf Auda), Francesco Quinn (Syed Ali), Michelle Forbes (Lynne Kresge)

"You consider going against the grain as some kind of virtue!" Tony Almeida

Timeframe

Key Events

11:00 P.M. The President, CTU and Kim all see the blast. The CTU chopper safely picks up Jack, but he can't reach Kim by phone.

11:05 P.M. Yusuf Auda, the Arab liaison, asks Tony if he can help the investigation. Tony doesn't trust him.

11:09 P.M. Tony determines that the tape is genuine and not spliced. Michelle says Ali denies the tape is real, but Carrie insists it is. Tony will present both opinions to the President.

11:12 P.M. Palmer learns Jack is safe. He hears the tape evidence and decides to call for an emergency session of Congress to formally declare war.

11:18 P.M. Michelle believes there is reasonable doubt about the tape.

11:20 P.M. The Joint Chiefs explain they can start strikes the same day. Prime Minister Barghouti asks the President not to rush into a response.

11:22 P.M. Jack is back at CTU and Ali is carried out. Michelle shares her concerns with Jack and asks him to interrogate Ali again.

11:25 P.M. Jack follows Ali out, tells him the truth about his son and asks for the truth about the tape. Ali confirms it is not real. A hidden sniper kills Ali with a single shot.

11:31 P.M. Jack is convinced Ali's murder means the tape is a fake and he fights with Tony about it.

11:34 P.M. Kim enters a convenience store to make a phone call, but is caught up in a robbery. Jack calls Palmer about Ali's murder and says the tape is fake. The President demands proof.

11:45 P.M. Palmer shares with Novick that he is concerned they are moving too fast towards war. Jack's phone rings and a man claiming to have created the tape and killed Ali demands Kate Warner.

11:55 P.M. Jack calls Michelle for help in proving the recording false.

11:57 P.M. Michelle and Jack find Kate and ask her to come with them urgently. Yusuf and Carrie see this and she calls Tony.

11:59 P.M. Tony tries to block Jack from leaving, but he is knocked out. Kate leaves with Jack.

Palmer consults with the Joint Chiefs on a video link.

Ali is shot dead by a sniper.

Tony confronts Jack and Kate.

Tony Almeida ends up spending a large chunk of the middle of season two on crutches due to an altercation with Jack Bauer at CTU. In reality, that injury spun out of a real life problem for actor Carlos Bernard. "Over Christmas break, I was in a basketball game and my ankle was broken and dislocated to the point where my foot was pointing in the wrong direction," the actor details. "I had to have surgery to have screws put in to hold it all together. When they jerked it back into place, it was one of the most painful moments of my life. So, I had all this stuff done over Christmas break and yet I was calling the producers saying, 'I sort of sprained my ankle, but I'll be okay, just on crutches for a bit.'

"Well, I had to be on crutches for three months, because if I had put any weight on the screws, I would have broken them. The first day back from Christmas, Jack and Tony are supposed

Research Files

Audio Authentication: The CTU agents work to get audio authentication for all the voices on the Cyprus conversations to prove or disprove their validity once and for all. The art of audio authentication is growing more prevalent in the digital age. Forensic experts are now trained to authenticate audio recordings in a number of ways. First, a technician can listen with headphones to the original tape or recording using high quality analytical equipment. The tech then examines recorded events and categorizes them as environmental or non-environmental. Lastly, critical listening gives an extensive audit of the foreground information. Also key is the physical inspection of the material focusing on tampering, followed by signs of magnetic development and the marks of any digital editing. Skilled examiners can uncover an amazing amount of evidence that can then be used to solve a variety of crimes, including kidnapping and extortion.

Additional Intel

Canadian native Elisha Cuthbert started her career modeling at the age of seven. She's fluent in French, as well as being a huge hockey enthusiast. She wrote a blog about the sport for the National Hockey League website during the 2005 season at: *www.nhl.com/blogcentral/cuthbert_blog.html*.

to have this knock down, drag out fight, falling down stairs and everything. It happens that Kiefer had previously broken his kneecap and so both of us are gimping around, so we staged this fight that was so lame," he laughs. "He basically just knocks me over and kicks my ankle — that's how they explained the injury!" Thus, Tony spends a lot of time at CTU leaning on crutches, out of the physical action. Bernard's misery was finally relieved towards the end of the season. "Three months later, we are still filming, and I convinced them to let me wrap up the 'Tony's injury' thing onscreen, so I could toss the crutches aside. I was so damn sick of those crutches!"

12:00 am - 1:00 am

Director: Jon Cassar
Writers: Evan Katz & Gil Grant

Guest Cast: Jude Ciccolella (Mike Novick), Alan Dale (Vice President Jim Prescott), Donnie Keshawarz (Yusuf Auda), Reiko Aylesworth (Michelle Dessler)

"We've got planes in the air. Either we're committed or not!" Vice President Prescott

Timeframe   Key Events

12:00 A.M. Jack explains to Kate that they are on the brink of war. He needs to take her to the caller.

12:04 A.M. Carrie tells Tony that Michelle may have helped Jack. Palmer, Lynne and Novick disembark Air Force One in LA. Palmer tells Vice President Prescott there may not be an attack, yet his advisors think it is too late.

12:07 A.M. Kim is in the middle of a shootout at the store.

12:09 A.M. Jack realizes they are being tailed by Yusuf, who offers to help him.

12:11 A.M. Tony confronts Michelle with Carrie's accusation.

12:19 A.M. Jack keeps Kate in the car. At the rendezvous, Jack meets Captain Jonathan Wallace. He explains he killed his unit and faked the Ali recording to start a war in the Middle East to increase the oil holdings of the people who hired him. Wallace now fears for his life, but Kate, a board member of Warner Industries, can get him out of the country. Wallace taps an electrical socket.

12:23 A.M. The socket turns out the neon light outside and signals a gunman to apprehend Kate. Yusuf saves her life and calls Jack to alert him.

12:31 A.M. Novick tries to contact Jack.

12:33 A.M. Carrie convinces Tony that Michelle is conspiring with Jack.

12:38 A.M. Yusuf secures the area for Kate.

12:44 A.M. Carrie redirects all of Michelle's outside communication to track on her computer. Novick briefs Palmer on Jack's improper activities and theorizes he may have snapped. Palmer trusts Jack and orders Novick to find him.

12:47 A.M. Jack is obliged to hand Kate over to Wallace to get the tape evidence.

12:56 A.M. Novick and Lynne meet with Vice President Prescott via videophone and discuss Palmer's sudden softness on the war. They mull the repercussions of trusting Jack.

12:58 A.M. Wallace puts Kate in his trunk, Yusuf tells Jack the tracker is in place. Shots are fired from the warehouse.

Kim tries to save a life.

Jack finds Captain Jonathan Wallace.

Novick, Lynne and Prescott plot against President Palmer.

One of the more powerful hallmarks of the series has always been its approach to writing stories which incorporate important racial issues without focusing or dwelling on them. Season two placed African American David Palmer in the Presidency, a historic milestone that hasn't yet occurred in reality in the US, yet the series never pandered to the fact. Joel Surnow says, "We just did it, and we don't think in those terms. Palmer is a great character and he was running for President, and he became President. We didn't stop to applaud ourselves for being politically correct. There have been black Presidents in movies before; and George Bush has had two black Secretaries of State and a National Security Advisor, so I don't think we are that far away from the election of a black President actually happening. If we had done this story in 1969, it might have been radical."

Executive producer Howard Gordon concurs, "It wasn't really by design, but by inference. This was hugely important, to me anyway; the idea of what America stands for. America stands for this possibility: that a country, which as recently as 120 years ago had enslaved blacks, had now healed itself to the point where a black man could lead the country. This is exactly what is great about America. As flawed as it is, it has the mechanisms to heal itself; and when you think about it, this was the culmination of that healing. It wasn't that grandiose of an idea [to have an African American President], but I think this was absolutely the implication, and gave the whole story a kind of power that it wouldn't have had if it was any white-haired character actor playing the President."

Research Files

Videophone: Novick and Lynne meet with Vice President Prescott via videophone. Once a dream of the future, videophones are now a common communication link in the business and technology worlds. Also known as videotelephony, the technology is mostly used in large corporate setups and military agencies to link national or global representatives for meetings, briefings or conferences. AT&T first conducted experiments of a 'Picturephone' product and service in the early 1960s. While videophones are still a novelty in the consumer world, they are becoming more popular with younger generations and through mobile technology. An off-shoot technology, the webcam, is also growing through personal computer use in which thousands of users world-wide conference using cheaply available webcams and microphones employed using software over the Internet.

Additional Intel

While 24 purports to be shown in 'real-time', each episode is actually only forty-four minutes long, not a full hour. However, the clock does continue to tick during credits and commercial breaks, and so it does achieve the final sixty minutes by the end of the episode.

1:00 am - 2:00 am

Director: Jon Cassar
Writers: Joel Surnow & Michael Loceff

Guest Cast: Reiko Aylesworth (Michelle Dessler), Lourdes Benedicto (Carrie Turner), Ted Sutton (General Blaye), Victor Rivers (Sergeant Amis)

"We're surrounded. We're running out of time."
Jack Bauer

Timeframe — Key Events

1:00 A.M. Jack pulls Kate from the trunk and into the warehouse. Jack, Yusuf and Wallace fight the snipers. Jack calls Michelle for satellite assistance.

1:05 A.M. Kim tells the police about the situation and her own charges.

1:06 A.M. Palmer sees news reports of chaos due to the bomb detonation. Carrie tells Tony about Michelle's activities.

1:15 A.M. Kim is taken to the station. Michelle hides her work from Carrie and Tony.

1:17 A.M. Michelle calls Jack from her PDA and sends him the warehouse map. Tony confronts her and she denies helping Jack.

1:20 A.M. Jack and Wallace figure out an escape route. Palmer orders that there be no pre-emptive strikes, giving Jack time to disprove the tape.

1:27 A.M. Jack, Kate, Wallace and Yusuf make a daring escape from the warehouse. Wallace is shot in the neck and Kate gives him first aid.

1:30 A.M. The President enacts a curfew and orders the National Guard to start making arrests. Michelle connects Tony with Jack and he explains Palmer ordered him to find proof about the tape. Tony tells Jack to bring Wallace to CTU. Jack refuses.

1:38 A.M. Sheriff's Sergeant Amis tells Kim that Gary was charged with Carla's murder.

1:40 A.M. Kate has a Warner jet prepped, but Wallace loses consciousness. Kim calls CTU and finds out her dad is alive. Jack takes Wallace to a clinic.

1:45 A.M. Kim calls Miguel who isn't happy to hear from her.

1:51 A.M. Michelle apologizes to Tony and he dismisses her.

1:53 A.M. The Joint Chiefs tell Palmer the bombers are on their way and chaos is building on US streets.

1:55 A.M. Wallace is dying. He is about to tell Jack where the source files are when he dies. Jack looks at his x-ray, cuts into Wallace and pulls out a microchip.

Jack calls Michelle for satellite assistance.

Miguel's fate is revealed.

Palmer and Novick plan for chaos.

Editor Scott Powell, who has been with *24* since episode three of the first season, details the issues with editing the show: "People often ask me if the real-time format makes it more difficult — and it does when you are structuring different scenes together. But the essence of what we do is going through the footage and constructing the individual scenes, and they are always shot in real time anyway. What makes it more challenging is the way they shoot it. They will set up a situation, block it and have the actors go through it, and the cameras are following them as if they are one of the characters. It may start as a wide-master shot, but then it will become an over-shoulder, then a close-up, and then an insert of someone picking up a piece of paper. They will do four different variations of that, and then turn the camera around and do it the other way. We then pick out all the little gems, to extract what has the best potential. It's

more like cutting a documentary in that way."

Reflecting on his work, Powell offers, "One of the great moments was a scene in season two where the sequence started in the middle of a shootout. The previous show ended — 'Boom, boom, boom!' — in a big shootout and everyone is attacked from the roofs of this alley and they are all ducking for cover... end of show. The next show then started — 'Bam, bam, bam!' — mid-gunfight and they all escape into this warehouse. Then there is this intense warehouse scene, and in the edit I'm popping in and out of boxes and I've got a character in the mirror, and there's all this chaos. Then it goes to a phone call to CTU, and Michelle is walking across the place in a box-wide, and there's a box-in-close, and then there is a third box where Jack is talking to her. It's one of the coolest pieces of editing that I think I've done."

Research Files

Microchip: Jack reviews Wallace's X-ray and digs out an implanted microchip from his body that contains the Cyprus audio files. A human microchip implant is an integrated circuit device encased in silicate glass. Typically, implants are used to store personal information resources like medical histories or contact information. It is also possible for implants to have GPS capability, so individuals can be physically located by latitude, longitude, speed, and direction of movement just through the chip. The term 'microchip' itself is used rather loosely; in electronics it specifically refers to the silicon semiconductor crystal.

Additional Intel

All of the *24* episodes are edited on an AVID/Symphony non-linear system. In season four, the show converted to HDTV format and upgraded to the AVID Nitrous system. Each episode takes about three weeks to construct, from the beginning of the edit to the final locked show.

Kate Warner

Experience:
Warner International Corporation

Education:
Stanford University – Bachelors of Science, Economics

Personal:
Single
Father – Robert Warner
Mother – deceased
Sister – Marie Warner

Sherry Palmer

Experience:

Congressional Spouses Club – President
USO World Board – Appointee
Congressional Wives for Human Rights –
        Fundraising Chairwoman
Maryland Hunger Fund – Chairman of the Board

Education:

Georgetown University – Bachelor of Arts, Sociology

Personal:

Divorced
Son – Keith Palmer
Daughter – Nicole Palmer

2:00 am - 3:00 am

Director: James Whitmore Jr.
Writer: Howard Gordon

Guest Cast: Tobin Bell (Peter Kingsley), Peter Outerbridge (Ronnie Stark), Nick Offerman (Marcus), Gregg Henry (Jonathan Wallace)

"He'll break." Stark

Timeframe — Key Events

2:00 A.M. Palmer explains that he is waiting on Jack Bauer's proof, but is persuaded a surprise first attack is necessary.

2:03 A.M. Yusuf examines the chip and finds a transponder.

2:05 A.M. Michelle gets a call from Tony that Jack has got the evidence. Jack takes the tracker to throw off the assassins, while Yusuf and Kate take the audio files and escape.

2:13 A.M. Tony calls the President with the news. Palmer wants to call off the attack.

2:17 A.M. Tony tells Michelle he called the President. Marie's henchman Ronnie Stark shoots Jack with a taser and drags him into the clinic.

2:25 A.M. Novick and Lynne realize that the Vice President has called a meeting. Stark is ordered by his superior, Peter Kingsley, to torture Jack to get the chip back.

2:30 A.M. Carrie and Michelle accuse each other of sabotaging their work. Tony calls Michelle into his office and she tells Tony how her brother, Danny, left his wife and children for Carrie, who then dumped him. Michelle receives a call — Danny is at CTU to see her.

2:33 A.M. When Danny sees Carrie he attacks her. Security guards pull him off while Michelle watches, horrified.

2:39 A.M. Carrie tells Tony that Chappelle is looking for him.

2:42 A.M. Stark continues his brutal work on Jack to no avail.

2:46 A.M. Novick tells Lynne that Prescott is invoking Section four of the Twenty-fifth Amendment on Palmer. He asks Lynne if she supports Palmer and she says yes. Novick says he can't and locks a shocked Lynne in a room.

2:53 A.M. Yusuf and Kate intend to head to CTU, but a group of racist men attack them.

2:56 A.M. Tony calls Chappelle, who says he is coming to CTU with key resources to help.

2:58 A.M. Stark beats Jack so badly that he stops breathing. Stark frantically administers CPR, and yells for his men to find epinephrine.

Racists attack Yusuf and Kate.

Jack is tortured...

... and stops breathing.

From the beginning, *24* has always been a series that intended to show the brutality associated with trying to stop terrorism. Jack Bauer's methods, from chopping off the finger of a thug to decapitating an informant, became increasingly violent over the course of the series. In the last third of season two, the tables were turned on Jack as he became the victim of actual death-inducing torture.

Producer Howard Gordon says that the memorable arc was necessary to show the depths to which Jack would sacrifice himself for the cause, and to show the level of pain he would be able to absorb. "Obviously, the idea that anybody would allow himself to be tortured to death — that was a measure of his mettle. It was pretty cool and we just knew we wanted to take it to a place where his heart actually gave out. So that much we knew, and we had to do it in a way that wasn't too

graphic and disturbing." Enduring beatings, injections and other sickeningly creative alternatives, a naked Jack Bauer was literally taken to the edge of his mortality. "Maybe it was a little over the top, but look, in the end, it killed him — at least until the next week," Gordon laughs. "That's all we knew. Yes, we had some issues with the network censors. But it's always more horrifying to lay the suggestion of something than to really see exactly what is happening. I think we saw the tool and the body part that was used and you sort of draw your own conclusions off-camera." The intensity of that arc was difficult for the entire production team, especially Kiefer Sutherland. "Oh, it was rough," relates Gordon. "I remember having some trouble with it, and it wasn't an easy time for anybody at that point. And Kiefer had some very strong opinions about it."

Research Files

Stun Guns: Jack is shot with a taser by Kingsley's thug Ronnie Stark. Stun guns deliver a series of millisecond-long electric shocks that cause the victim's muscles to contract, immobilizing him. A popular variation of the standard stun gun is the taser, which fires two metal darts, connected via metal wires to the stun gun, allowing the user to stun from a greater distance (though you only get one shot!). The technology was developed in the early 1970s as a non-lethal way for police to incapacitate violent criminals. While companies that make stun guns and tasers specify that the weapons should be used only for self-defense or incapacitating an unruly person, they are used as torture devices in many parts of the world. Electrical incapacitation is an extremely painful and effective means by which to immobilize someone.

Additional Intel

The intensity and graphic nature of Jack's torture in this episode earned it the Parents Television Council's (a family-viewing watchdog) least family-friendly program citation for the week.

3:00 am - 4:00 am

Director: James Whitmore Jr.
Writer: Neil Cohen

Guest Cast: Reiko Aylesworth (Michelle Dessler), Tobin Bell (Peter Kingsley), Glenn Morshower (Agent Aaron Pierce), Donnie Keshawarz (Yusuf Auda)

"Don't thank me. I just don't have anyone to take your place right now." Ryan Chappelle

Timeframe

3:00 A.M. A doctor is forced to administer epinephrine and Jack is revived. On Kingsley's orders Stark is shot by another henchman, O'Hara.

3:05 A.M. Novick tells Prescott he has taken care of Lynne.

3:08 A.M. The men rob the bloodied Yusuf of his money and the chip. Kate begs for the chip, offering money, but they pile into her car.

3:11 A.M. O'Hara makes the doctor inject Jack with Beroglide. Jack asks the doctor for help while O'Hara takes another call from Kingsley.

3:18 A.M. Chappelle arrives and commends Tony. Tony says Jack was right. Chappelle tells Tony he won't support him as permanent Director of CTU if he takes Jack's side.

3:20 A.M. Lynne starts a fire and escapes, but falls over the stair railing and is unconscious. Palmer asks Secret Service Agent Pierce if Prescott is planning behind his back.

3:25 A.M. Jack hyperventilates from the drug, so he offers to tell O'Hara what he wants. The doctor slams the syringe into O'Hara and Jack grabs his gun and shoots him and the other men. Jack gets Peter Kingsley's name from O'Hara.

3:33 A.M. Novick warns Prescott that Palmer is suspicious.

3:36 A.M. Jack calls Michelle at CTU, but the signal is lost. Palmer admits to Novick that he doesn't trust Prescott and then they learn of Lynne's fall. Novick is panicked.

3:42 A.M. Michelle gets a general trace of Jack's location and tells Tony. Carrie observes them. Jack drives to the meeting place and finds a dying Yusuf who tells him Kate has the chip.

3:45 A.M. The men demand money from Kate.

3:52 A.M. Carrie tries to extort Tony. He exposes her plan to Chappelle who dismisses her and then admonishes Tony.

3:55 A.M. Kate tries to exchange money for the chip, but the men want her. She runs and Jack shows up. Jack tries to get the chip from the men.

3:59 A.M. Prescott hosts the Cabinet to determine if they should relieve Palmer of the Presidency.

Key Events

Lynne falls over the stair railing.

Jack gets back the upper hand.

Prescott hosts the Cabinet to relieve Palmer.

One of the most compelling arcs of the last third of the season was the introduction of the Twenty-fifth Amendment storyline, which had President Palmer being tried by his Cabinet to determine if he was fit to hold office, due to his hesitancy in starting a retaliatory war. As has happened before, it was a storyline that wasn't part of the initial plans for the season. Executive producer Howard Gordon admits, "Oh, no, desperation is the mother of invention! We were at the place we find ourselves at least once and sometimes two or three times a season, where we just have no idea what to do. We got really tired of chasing the nuclear bomb and its components from mosque to warehouse to bookie joint, and we got tired of writing it. In the wake of that fatigue, we came up with the idea of exploding the nuke and, 'Let's tell the story of retribution' and 'Now what?'" The 'now what?' became the invoking of the Twenty-fifth Amendment against Palmer. "We figured there must be a provision somewhere for a

President who is mentally incapable of carrying out his duties, and lo and behold there existed the Twenty-fifth Amendment. Of course, it was accelerated beyond any realistic time frame, but we tried to sell it as credibly as possible. The Twenty-fifth Amendment was bent a little bit, but the intent was there."

Gordon says that storyline also helped flesh out the simmering hostilities against Palmer from his enemies within his own administration. "I think what I found interesting was that the subtext of race was always present. The idea that there probably had been people gunning for him from the beginning, literally and metaphorically, got to be expressed a little bit here, so loyalties could be tested and betrayals put into relief. I loved it. It was one of those things where we found this idea [of the Twenty-fifth Amendment], and were grateful as hell for it saving us. It was the first time we got to do really good political stuff. We had done a lot of soap opera stuff with the Palmer White House, so this was the first time we got to play a palace coup, much like Julius Caesar."

Research Files

Epinephrine: Jack is injected with epinephrine when he goes into cardiac arrest from the intense torture. Epinephrine (sometimes referred to as 'epi'), or adrenaline, is a hormone and a neurotransmitter. It was isolated and identified in 1895 by Napoleon Cybulski and first artificially synthesized in 1904 by Friedrich Stolz. Epinephrine plays a central role in the short-term stress reaction — the biological response to threatening or exciting conditions. In general, it increases heart rate, elevates the blood sugar level, dilates the pupils, and constricts arterioles in the skin and gut while dilating arterioles in leg muscles. It is commonly used to revive cardiac arrest patients. The other drug referenced, Beroglide, is a fictional drug created by the writers for the torture scenes.

Additional Intel

After almost twenty years appearing as a guest and recurring actor on more than thirty television series, *24* marked actor Dennis Haysbert's first regular cast member role on a show. His portrayal of David Palmer has earned him three Image Award nominations, and a Golden Globe nomination.

4:00 am - 5:00 am

Director: Ian Toynton

Writers: Robert Cochran & Howard Gordon

Guest Cast: Robert Pine (Secretary of Agriculture), John Rubinstein (Secretary of State), Austin Tichenor (Secretary of the Treasury)

> "I'm the President, Mike. You don't call me by my first name." President David Palmer

Timeframe

Key Events

4:00 A.M. Jack breaks down the door and retrieves the chip.

4:04 A.M. Novick admits to Palmer that the Cabinet members are debating if he is fit to serve as Chief Executive. Palmer walks into the conference room and Prescott tells Palmer they are invoking the Twenty-fifth Amendment. The Secretary of State gives Palmer the chance to explain himself.

4:15 A.M. Tony says Palmer called off the attack an hour ago, but Chappelle says the White House may reinstate it. Michelle gets a call from Jack about the chip.

4:18 A.M. Prescott brings reporter Ron Wieland in to testify against Palmer.

4:20 A.M. Michelle finds the chip has been damaged. Tony gets a call from Kim and he is finally able to connect her to Jack.

4:23 A.M. Palmer confronts Novick on his betrayal.

4:29 A.M. Prescott calls Roger Stanton against Palmer.

4:32 A.M. Video footage of Stanton's torture is played for the group. Palmer attempts to defend himself. Chappelle informs Prescott that Jack has the evidence and Palmer has a new chance.

4:37 A.M. Tony and Michelle work the files.

4:42 A.M. Kate is upset and Jack consoles her. His phone rings. Michelle tells him the name of the hacker who probably made the files, Alex Hewitt. Jack gets an address.

4:45 A.M. Jack talks to Palmer and explains he is going to find the evidence.

4:47 A.M. Prescott calls for a vote on Palmer, despite Jack's promise.

4:53 A.M. Tony tells Jack he can't find a connection between Hewitt and Kingsley. The Cabinet splits the vote and the Secretary of State goes against Palmer, who is escorted out.

4:58 A.M. Prescott is sworn in as President.

4:59 A.M. Jack finds Hewitt's loft and hears someone else arrive — Sherry Palmer.

The final vote is cast.

Palmer is escorted out.

Prescott is sworn in as President.

Mark Marcum, the computer video supervisor, is responsible for the team that handles all the video screens and technology used onscreen in the series. One of their most complicated contributions to the show was Palmer's Twenty-fifth Amendment trial. "When that big wall opens up and there are six different people talking all at the same time, that was all done live and completely interactively," he explains. "There was no videotape. The six actors were in six different sets with six cameras on them. We had a big technical switcher in the back where we were able to switch the images around. They were all able to hear each other, and they actually acted the scenes with Dennis live. It was very cool."

Another important function of their department is setting up what is called the "poor man's process". *24* features a large number of scenes in cars, which look real but are actually stationary

vehicles with video footage (or plates) projected on a screen behind them, to give the illusion of actual driving. "[DP] Rodney Charters came up with the idea and we made it happen," Marcum details. "We do all the car work live, there's no green screen here. My department does all the technical side of those plates: we shoot them and play them back. We are one of the few shows that do it regularly. It's better for production, and I think everyone likes it better. We started it in season one because they are in cars so much. Also, half the show takes place in the middle of the night and unless you want to switch the whole crew over to working nights for four months, which is really hard on them, you try to figure out how to do splits, where you come to work at noon and work until dark on one thing, and then go outside and do your night work. With this, you can take the car work with you anywhere. We've done it in airplane hangers and in warehouses, and on locations where you can fill up three hours of the daylight, and therefore not end up working all night."

Research Files

Twenty-fifth Amendment: The Cabinet and Secretary of State invoke the Twenty-fifth Amendment with the intent of ousting Palmer from office for not backing the war. The actual amendment was passed two years after JFK's assassination, to clarify an ambiguous provision of the Constitution regarding succession to the Presidency. It also establishes procedures both for filling a vacancy in the office of the Vice President, as well as responding to Presidential disabilities. The Senate passed the amendment (then known as 'Senate Joint Resolution 1') by a unanimous, seventy-two to zero vote. Wisconsin and Nebraska were the first states to ratify it. Often Presidents who are temporarily rendered incapable of performing their jobs due to surgeries or medical conditions will invoke the Twenty-fifth until they are fit to retain office again.

Additional Intel

Before appearing as Vice President Jim Prescott in *24*, actor Alan Dale was best known to Australian and British TV audiences as another, very different Jim: the long suffering Jim Robinson in the hit Australian soap *Neighbours*. The New Zealander has also appeared in *E.R.*, *The X-Files* and *The O.C.*

5:00 am - 6:00 am

Director: Ian Toynton

Writers: Virgil Williams & Duppy Demetrius

Guest Cast: Lourdes Benedicto (Carrie Turner), Billy Burke (Gary Matheson), Jude Ciccolella (Mike Novick), Rick D. Wasserman (Alex Hewitt)

"I'll handle Agent Bauer, he won't be a problem. He's very low on the food chain." Sherry Palmer

Jack confronts Sherry.

Michelle and Tony drug Chappelle.

Jack helps Kim in a crisis.

Timeframe | Key Events

5:00 A.M. Jack secretly watches Sherry. Prescott orders they proceed with the attack. Novick collects Palmer's war key codes.

5:04 A.M. Chappelle explains the new chain of command and orders Tony not to expend anymore time on Jack.

5:06 A.M. Jack knocks out Sherry's bodyguard and demands to know what she is doing there. She refuses to answer and he fires his gun at her. Jack discovers Hewitt behind the wall and forces him to talk.

5:14 A.M. Hewitt says he will only speak to Sherry as she has promised to protect him. Sherry admits she was out for revenge on Palmer and demands immunity from Jack.

5:19 A.M. Palmer asks Agent Pierce for help contacting Jack.

5:21 A.M. Carrie tells Chappelle she thinks Tony and Michelle are working with Jack.

5:27 A.M. Jack calls Tony and updates him. He requests a chopper to bring Hewitt in. Sherry promises the hacker immunity.

5:30 A.M. Tony asks Chappelle for the chopper for Jack. Chappelle orders Tony to step down. Hewitt gathers his audio material and then grows suspicious of Sherry.

5:39 A.M. Palmer calls Tony to talk to Jack. He connects them. Jack explains Sherry's involvement and Hewitt's evidence.

5:42 A.M. Jack demands the helicopter from Tony. Under police care, Kim packs her things from the Matheson house. Gary hides in the house.

5:46 A.M. Michelle and Tony drug Chappelle so they can get the chopper for Jack.

5:51 A.M. Jack tells Sherry that Prescott is now President and she is shocked. Tony calls Jack.

5:54 A.M. Gary takes out the cop and seeks Kim to kill her. She cracks him with a can and gets his gun and cell phone.

5:56 A.M. Kim calls Jack, she is terrified. Jack has to talk her through shooting Gary dead. Jack calls Kate to get Kim. Hewitt tries to escape and stabs Sherry. Jack pursues him.

Story editor Duppy Demetrius started working on *24* during the second season. Episode twenty-two became his début script, co-written with then-story editor, Virgil Williams. "I was surprised that we were given such a big responsibility for that season. It was a big turnaround episode," says Demetrius. Reflecting on the script, he says there are two scenes that really stand out for him. The first being: "Kim manages to knock Gary out and then calls Jack to have someone come get her. While she's doing this, Gary wakes up and starts for her again. It's here that Jack tells Kim to shoot Gary. She doesn't want to, but Jack insists. She does, and lays Gary out. She starts to lower her gun when — and this is my favorite part — Jack says, 'Shoot him again.' She does. This whole sequence is a tense thriller, and, I think, a great *24* moment.

"As for the most satisfying part of the script, I'd say that it's the

Jack/Sherry Palmer story. Jack has followed a lead to the man — Alex Hewitt — who is responsible for fabricating the Cyprus recordings. Alex is the only person who can testify that the recordings are false, thereby stopping the United States from waging war on the Middle East. Jack is searching Hewitt's place when Sherry Palmer enters with ideas of her own on what to do about Alex Hewitt. It's here that Jack and Sherry face off and are forced to work together, as Alex doesn't want to cooperate with either of them. This whole story arc is key in getting to and, ultimately, taking out the man behind everything. It was probably my favorite scene to write because of the subtleties that were involved with Hewitt, who, for the most part, is a loose cannon, and ready to snap. It was satisfying to see it all come together and further the story in such a dramatic way."

Research Files

Hacker: Michelle traces the chip programming to a hacker named Alex Hewitt. A hacker is a tag associated with someone who is extremely proficient with computers. Back in the 1970s, hacker was a term given to those who knew how to write code. During the 1980s and 1990s it was a term meant for those who worked their way through computer systems, without approval, rewriting code or creating viruses. According to the *Urban Dictionary*, there are three main kinds of hacker today: White Hats, those who hack for the enjoyment of exploration and knowledge; Black Hats (crackers), those who hack to find and exploit system weaknesses; and Grey Hats, those that do a bit of both.

Additional Intel

24 has a production cycle which is unique in the television world. The vast majority of scripted one-hour dramas are shot on an eight-day cycle. From the beginning, it was decided that *24* would shoot episodes on a more efficient fifteen-day cycle, making two episodes at once.

6:00 am - 7:00 am

Director: Jon Cassar

Writers: Gil Grant & Evan Katz

Guest Cast: Randle Mell (Brad Hammond), Paul Schulze (Ryan Chappelle), Alan Dale (Vice President Jim Prescott), Tobin Bell (Peter Kingsley)

"Make no mistake about it, I do what I have to do." Jack Bauer

Timeframe Key Events

6:00 A.M. Brad Hammond from Division calls for Chappelle but Tony deflects him.

6:03 A.M. Jack chases Hewitt, trying to cut a deal in exchange for stopping the war.

6:05 A.M. Kingsley finds out Hewitt is gone and worries he could blow their whole operation. Hewitt pulls a gun and Jack shoots him in the leg.

6:17 A.M. Counselor Brian Jacobs arrives for Palmer and they talk about appeals. Palmer gives him Kingsley's name as the orchestrator of events. Michelle leaves CTU to find Jack. Hammond locks down CTU.

6:20 A.M. Jacobs appeals to Novick to let them build the case against Kingsley. He eventually agrees and provides access to the database. Carrie finds Chappelle.

6:28 A.M. Novick asks Palmer to help them request airspace access from Turkey's Prime Minister.

6:30 A.M. Jack insists Sherry help him get to Kingsley. Jack has heart pain.

6:32 A.M. Kingsley guarantees his associate Max that Hewitt will be eliminated. Michelle gets onto Hewitt's computer to access his audio archive, but is arrested by CTU agents before she and Jack can get the right files.

6:41 A.M. Palmer is connected to Turkey. Kate finds Kim and is able to convince the terrified girl Jack sent her.

6:45 A.M. Michelle and Tony sit imprisoned in a CTU holding room.

6:54 A.M. Jack makes Sherry call Kingsley, demanding the tapes of their conversations. Jack plays back the generator of Hewitt's voice to trick Kingsley. They set up a meeting place.

6:56 A.M. Kingsley says he has no choice but to meet Sherry so he can get Hewitt.

6:59 A.M. Jack drives Sherry to the meeting, but he seizes up and the car careens off the road into an embankment in the riverbed basin.

Jack shoots Hewitt.

Michelle and Tony are imprisoned.

Jack has an attack.

Over the course of the second season, Tony made a dramatic journey: becoming a leader at CTU and a strong ally of Jack Bauer. Detailing that character evolution, executive producer Howard Gordon says, "Tony was a character who absolutely was reinvented on the fly. In some ways, Tony was two different characters. In the first year, he was very much a foil for Jack. They were two points of a triangle, with Nina as the third. Tony had more of a snarl in that first year," he laughs. "We just liked him; and his fate and place in the show always came in the margins of our discussions. Carlos always delivered so beautifully that his character took on a life of his own. We looked for and found opportunities to draw more out of him, and in many ways to draw him closer to the orbit of Jack Bauer. Having once been romantic and professional adversaries, they really became close colleagues."

"Part of the journey for Tony was that he was such a by-the-book

guy," Carlos Bernard adds. "I think part of his lesson was learning when to bend the rules. In the second season, he took out Chappelle to aid Jack in his efforts. It was a pretty dangerous move for him, and another moment of change for the character. He decided he had to break the rules now, and would do that time and time again throughout the rest of the seasons."

As to the fate of Tony, Bernard laughs and says he was always dreading the untimely death of his character. "It's always a concern, when it comes towards the end of a season especially. You know some bodies are going drop and so it is a worry. Throughout the first season I was concerned; but through the second season I learned not to worry about it. You think about it from time to time, but there is nothing you can do. But the way the story was structured, it seemed pretty clear that I was going to live through the end of the second season."

Research Files

Turkey: Prescott goes to Palmer to ask for his assistance in talking to Turkey about using their airspace to complete their attack. The Republic of Turkey is a part of the United Nations. Located mainly in Anatolia, with seven percent of its land located in the Balkans, it's often considered to be a part of Europe due to its cultural and political characteristics, but it's actually a transcontinental country straddling the Europe-Asia border. It was established on 29 October 1923 from the remnants of the Ottoman Empire. Turkey's capital is Ankara, but the largest city is Istanbul. There have been many governmental coups during the country's history and it is prone to severe earthquakes.

Additional Intel

Season two rounded out with another huge body count with more than 113 deaths captured on screen. A large chunk of those deaths were CTU employees in the explosion, and various random thugs; but deaths of note include Reza Naiyeer, Yusuf Auda and the heroic George Mason.

7:00 am - 8:00 am

Director: Jon Cassar
Story: Robert Cochran and Howard Gordon
Teleplay: Joel Surnow & Michael Loceff

Guest Cast: Reiko Aylesworth (Michelle Dessler), Eugene Robert Glazer (Alexander Trepkos), Laura Harris (Marie Warner), Jude Ciccolella (Mike Novick)

> "It's like this, either fire me, or get outta my chair."
> Tony Almeida

Timeframe	Key Events

7:00 A.M. Jack is trapped by his belt and Sherry leaves the car telling him she has to take care of herself. Jack pleads with Sherry and he wins her over.

7:03 A.M. Jacobs shows Novick a file on Kingsley connecting him to Wallace. Prescott prepares for the attacks.

7:06 A.M. Kingsley calls Max looking for Alex Hewitt. Chappelle demands Tony and Michelle connect him with Jack. They agree if their charges are dropped. Jack and Sherry hijack a car.

7:13 A.M. Kate and Kim arrive at CTU.

7:17 A.M. Chappelle contacts Jack and tells him he has full CTU support. Jack can't wait but wants a live audio feed with the President.

7:19 A.M. Jack wires Sherry with a transmitter.

7:24 A.M. Novick alerts Prescott about the Kingsley link, which will exonerate the Middle Eastern countries backing Second Wave. Novick says that Jack will get a live audio confession from Kingsley.

7:28 A.M. Palmer is connected to the live feed and is shocked that Sherry is involved too. Sherry walks into the LA Coliseum.

7:34 A.M. With Jack in the stands, Sherry gets Kingsley to confess the plan.

7:37 A.M. Kingsley doesn't believe Sherry has Hewitt and orders her killed. Nothing happens because Jack already took out the snipers. Jack is almost taken down, but CTU SWAT arrives and shoots Kingsley.

7:42 A.M. Prescott orders the attack to be aborted.

7:47 A.M. Max is informed Kingsley is dead and the war is called off, so he calls someone with a go-ahead. The Cabinet reinstates Palmer as President.

7:52 A.M. Chappelle gives Tony his job back.

7:56 A.M. At a press conference, Palmer pronounces the nation safe again. As he passes through the crowd, Mandy the assassin shakes his hand. She walks away, peels off latex and calls Max: "It's done."

7:59 A.M. The flesh on Palmer's hand is eaten away and he collapses.

Kingsley's last stand.

Jack and Kim reunite.

Palmer is infected.

After twenty-four hours involving terrorists on US soil, a nuclear bomb detonation and the temporary loss of his Presidency, it seemed like David Palmer's day couldn't get any worse... until the finale. The producers unveiled the ultimate cliffhanger with the poisoning of Palmer by Mandy the assassin in the final moments of the season. Joel Surnow says, "We thought we needed something tragic to end the season, as we do every season. We liked the Palmer idea and then thought what better person to do it than Mandy?"

Howard Gordon says the ending was a leap of faith for the team in terms of determining the actual future of David Palmer. "It was always supposed to be him. Although, the assassination attempt on him was, in a sense, a bit of a cheesy cliffhanger. We knew it was a surprising moment and obviously an ironic one given all the things he'd been through, only to have this cap the

season. It's something we would not normally have done, but we honestly didn't know in that moment whether he would be back. We had a story, but we didn't know. The tricky part is that we wrap the season and then have to make deals with actors and all these business things. We can't commit to an actor if we don't have a story for them, so we had to allow ourselves the flexibility and, in that moment, also take the chance that he wouldn't be available for the next season, even if we came up with an idea. Fortunately, we did, and moved on very quickly and had him survive that attempt." Did Haysbert initially respond badly to the script revelation? Gordon laughs, "Oh God yes, to the extent that Dennis ever freaks out. You get that sort of big, lazy kind of disapproval, I don't know how else to describe it. About as far as freaking out gets for Dennis is a big 'huh?'."

Research Files

Flesh-Eating Infection: Mandy the assassin passes a nasty flesh-eating substance to President Palmer via a latex appliance on her hand. In reality, necrotizing fasciitis is a rare but very serious infection that affects the skin. Usually caused by streptococcus bacteria, it is one of the fastest-spreading infections known, and tissue may be consumed at a rate of three centimetres per hour. It has a mortality rate of around twenty percent. The disease is diagnosed through blood cultures or seeping from the skin. Patients with necrotizing fasciitis typically have a fever and appear very ill. The affected skin is very painful, red or violet, and is swollen and hot to the touch. Early medical treatment is critical and often includes intravenous penicillin, and sometimes surgery.

Additional Intel

This episode marks the third time that the end of episode clock ticked silently, being replaced instead by the sound of President David Palmer's heartbeat as the show faded to black...

THE CLOCK'S
STILL TICKING...

24 DECLASSIFIED
THE COUNTDOWN IS ON

After the war on terror began the government declassified these early CTU missions so new agents could learn to combat threats the way Jack Bauer always had . . .

With extreme courage and skill!

24 DECLASSIFIED: OPERATION HELL GATE
by Marc Cerasini
0-06-084224-5/$6.99/$9.99 Can

24 DECLASSIFIED: VETO POWER
by John Whitman
0-06-084225-3/$6.99/$9.99 Can

24 DECLASSIFIED: TROJAN HORSE
by Marc Cerasini
0-06-084226-1/$6.99/$9.99 Can

Don't Miss
24 DECLASSIFIED: CAT'S CLAW by John Whitman
Coming in January 2007

PlayStation 2

24™

THE GAME

MARKSMAN, CLOSE-COMBAT EXPERT, RUTHLESS INTERROGATOR, HIGH-SPEED DRIVER, COUNTER-TERRORISM AGENT AND PROTECTIVE FATHER. CAN YOU FILL JACK BAUER'S SHOES?_

PlayStation 2

WWW.24-THEGAME.COM

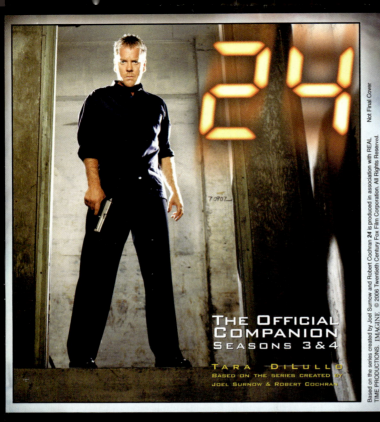
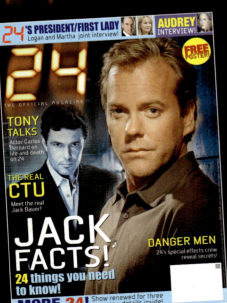